MEMORIES OF MANCHESTER

TRUE NORTH BOOKS
DEAN CLOUGH
HALIFAX
WEST YORKSHIRE
HX3 5AX
TEL 01422 344344

The Publishers would like to thank the following companies for supporting the production of this book

Main Sponsor

Lancashire Dairies Limited

J ALLCOCK & SONS LIMITED

GEC ALSTOM

THE ARNDALE CENTRE

BRITISH AEROSPACE REGIONAL AIRCRAFT

ERNEST BROADBELT LIMITED

CHETHAM'S SCHOOL OF MUSIC

CIBA SPECIALITY CHEMICALS PLC

CON LLOYD LIMITED

DALE & COMPANY (ANCOATS) LIMITED

DEGUSSA LIMITED

THE DUCKWORTH GROUP

F DUERR & SONS LIMITED

LOUIS DUFFY

ELCOMETER INSTRUMENTS LIMITED

FORSYTHE BROTHERS LIMITED

WILLIAM GRIMSHAW & SONS LIMITED

G-MEX

H MARCEL GUEST LIMITED

HAUSER LIMITED

ITAC LIMITED

MANCHESTER HIGH SCHOOL FOR GIRLS

A MAYNE & SON LIMITED

J MILLS CONTRACTORS LIMITED

PALACE THEATRE

PROCTER & GAMBLE LIMITED

H & J QUICK LIMITED

RHODIA LIMITED

JOHN STANIAR & COMPANY LIMITED

TENNANTS (LANCASHIRE) LIMITED

TILL & WHITEHEAD LIMITED

UMIST

J & B WILDE & SONS

WILLIAMS MOTOR COMPANY (HOLDING) LIMITED

THE YANG SING RESTAURANT

First published in Great Britain by True North Books
Dean Clough
Halifax HX3 5AX
1998

ISBN 1 900 463 27 X

Introduction

Part of Manchester's victory celebrations

Welcome to *Memories of Manchester*, a look back on some of the places, events and people in the city which have shaped the lives of local people over a period of around half a century. The following pages are brought to life by a selection of images from the not-too-distant past, chosen according to their ability to rekindle memories of days gone by and show how people used to shop, work and play in the area where they grew up. Modern image reproduction techniques have enabled us to present these pictures in a way rarely seen before, and the lively design and informative text has attempted to set the book apart from some of the other works available.

The chosen period is one which generally contains events within the memory of a large number of people in Manchester - this is not a book about crinolines or bowler-hats! Neither is *Memories of Manchester* a work of local history in the normal sense of the term. It has far more to do with entertainment than serious study, but we hope you will agree it is none the worse for that. It is hoped that the following pages will prompt readers own memories of Manchester from days gone by - and we are always delighted to hear from people who can add to the information contained in the captions so that we can enhance future editions of the book.

Many local companies and organisations have allowed us to study their archives and include their history - and fascinating reading it makes too. The present-day guardians of the firms concerned are proud of their products, the achievements of their people and the hard work of their forefathers whose efforts created these long established organisations in the first place. We are pleased to play our part by making it possible for them to share their history with a wider audience.

When we began compiling *Memories of Manchester* several months ago we anticipated that the task would be a pleasurable one, but our expectations were greatly surpassed. There is a growing appetite for all things 'nostalgic' and we are pleased to have played a small part in swelling the number of images and associated information available to the growing number of enthusiasts.

There is much talk in modern times about the regeneration of the local economy, the influx of new industries and the challenge of attracting new enterprise from other regions to Manchester. And quite right too. We could, however, make the mistake of thinking that the changes are all happening *now*, but the reality is that there have always been major developments going on in the city. 'Change' is relentless and the photographs on the pages in the book serve to remind us of some of them.

Memories of Manchester has been a pleasure to compile, we sincerely hope you enjoy reading it.

Happy memories!

PHOTOGRAPH COMPILATION/COVER DESIGN...MARK SMITH

CAPTION RESEARCH AND COMPILATION..PEGGY BURNS

DESIGNERS...................MANDY WALKER, NICKY BRIGHTON AND CHRISTINE GALE

COPYWRITER..PAULINE BELL

BUSINESS DEVELOPMENT EDITORS......ALAN EASTHAM AND STUART GLENHOLMES

CONTENTS

Around the city centre

Manchester Central Library: Local Studies Unit

On-street parking was allowed in King Street in 1958, a boon no doubt to shoppers who could still find a parking place outside the store of their choice on rainy days such as this one. Does Manchester really have more rain than other places in the country, or does it merely seem so? The driver of the sleek drop head coupe at the kerbside was no doubt grateful for the cover it was giving him today. Raincoats were the order of the day, but look closely at the man wearing a hat on the left of the picture.

Surely he's wearing a Pac-a-mac. Remember Pac-a-macs? Where did they disappear to? And why? The fold away plastic raincoats were popular with men and women alike, and no one would have thought of leaving the house on a doubtful day without the ubiquitous mac in one's pocket or handbag. The mac probably fell as a victim of fashion; perhaps it became 'uncool' to wear a plastic mac. But such sensible and practical rainwear should definitely be resurrected.

Manchester Central Library: Local Studies Unit

Above: It was 1946 when this view of Piccadilly was captured from the second floor of Lewis's, and a tram and two buses which wear the distinctive livery of Manchester Corporation pass the famous department store.

Tramways were very expensive to construct, and the city's fleet of electric trams were destined within a few years to give way to the petrol driven motor bus and the trolley bus.

Surprisingly, trolley buses had been introduced to Greater Manchester before the First World War. They were faster and much quieter than the rattling trams, and because they could use a lot of the same electrical fixtures as trams many of the expensive tracks were abandoned and trolleys began to replace Manchester tram services as early as 1938.

The 1940s were the busiest time for bus and trolley bus operators, as even after the war was over petrol rationing kept most private cars off the roads. The 1990s saw exciting new developments in public transport; the Queen opened the popular new Metrolink service in 1992.

Right: It is rush hour in 1953, and hordes of weary commuters pass Horne's corner as they make their way to their bus stop at the end of a hard day's work. Yet another traffic jam is building up in Market Street, and it is interesting to note the cause of it. Two cars face each other nose to nose across the carriageway while a queue of traffic patiently (or perhaps impatiently, who knows?) waits for the drivers to sort it out. But it looks as though neither of them is intending to give way to the other. Are the two of them honking their horns, or hurling abuse, or casting ill mannered doubts on each other's parentage? Did this incident spark off the very first 'road rage' attack known to man? Did they get it sorted - or are they still there?

Left: What was a scene of bomb damage and devastation in 1941 has, by the time this photograph was taken in 1950, been cleared and flattened and put to good use as a car park. Some interesting vehicles can be identified here: from left to right in the foreground are a Ford 10, then a 12hp or possibly 14hp Vauxhall, and alongside it stands the very popular Austin 10. The car next to the Austin is a Wolseley; in its heyday this motor could be identified by the smallest child as being the model used most often by the police force, especially in London. The lighter car alongside is an Austin. The car with the divided windscreen behind the Austin 10 is yet another Austin, this time probably a Sheerline (or maybe a Princess). In the 1970s you might have picked an Austin Sheerline up for as little as a fiver until the car acquired 'collectable' status, after which the price began to rise. The Old Wellington Inn in the background, an inn built somewhere around 1328, was very fortunate to survive the 1940-41 blitz. It now takes pride of place in the modern pedestrianised area that characterises the Old Shambles.

Below: A view that was still new in 1958, when this photograph was taken. The popular old shops of Corporation Street and Market Street have disappeared and the new development in the typical 'square block' style of the sixties and seventies is in the process of construction. Not everything in the area fell to the developers, however; fortunately the redevelopment stopped short of the Cotton Exchange. It was a great pity that the Cross Street frontage of the Exchange had to be extended in 1921, when increasing demands of business demanded a larger trading floor. The beautiful classical colonnade and many steps to the front entrance gave the building an almost regal air that was lost with the new extension. When the Exchange was closed in 1968 a new use was found for the building and it became a centre for the performing arts. An auditorium was installed within the Great Hall for The Royal Exchange Theatre Company, its avant-garde glass and steel structure squatting within the ornate marble hall like an alien landing craft in the palace of Queen Victoria. Mancunians have learned to live with all the changes, though they haven't always liked them....

This pigeon's eye view of Bridge Street in 1957 was taken from one of the tax offices; as an aside, readers might remember the letter bomb addressed to the premises in the early 1990s that exploded causing a considerable amount of damage. Bridge Street, which leads on towards John Dalton Street, takes its name from the old bridge that took traffic across the River Irwell in the 18th Century. On the right of the photograph is the Masonic Hall which was built on the site of the Queens Theatre, its distinctive style of architecture revealing that it was built in 1931. The clock tower of the Town Hall dominates the skyline. Designed by Alfred Waterhouse in the 13th Century Gothic style, the Town Hall was constructed from Spinkwell stone quarried in Bradford, West Yorkshire, and was completed in 1868. The church-like archway at the top right hand side of the picture is the rear of the John Rylands Library in Deansgate. John Rylands was a leading Manchester cotton trader, and also a devout Christian man who devoted much of his later life to promoting evangelical education. After his death in 1888 Enriqueta, his third wife, constructed the large theological library in his memory.

Right: Piccadilly bus station has been in service for longer than anyone can remember, its trams, motor buses and trolley buses picking up and dropping commuters, shoppers and visitors to the city centre since the early years of the 20th Century. Public transport in the city has an even longer history, however; it was as long ago as 1824 when a Pendleton tollkeeper, John Greenwood, started a horse omnibus service along a three mile stretch of road between Pendleton Toll Gate and Market Street in Manchester city centre. Greenwood's omnibus service ran three times a day and was the first true bus service in Britain if not in the whole world. By 1850 the city had 64 omnibuses, and from around the 1860s horse-drawn trams made their appearance. Experiments were made with steam trams, a small locomotive replacing the horses. Pollution was an obvious problem, and local byelaws demanded that the locomotives 'consume their own smoke'. How - or if - this was done does not seem to have been recorded. With the building of the Metrolink service the city that thought it had seen the last tram in 1949 has come full circle.

Below: When plans for the Mancunian Way were conceived, hopes were high that the 'highway in the sky' would be the solution to Manchester's growing traffic problem, keeping the flow of vehicles out of the city centre. The new highway, built 20ft above ground level on stilts across the city, though providing some answers to problems did not end up fulfilling its earlier promise. On the skyline is the imposing domed clock tower of the Refuge Insurance Building which was designed by Paul Waterhouse, son of the famous architect Alfred Waterhouse. The building is now the Palace Hotel. On the skyline towards the right hand side of the photograph stands the chimney of the Dickenson Street Power Station, which was still supplying steam heating for UMIST, among other premises until the late 1980s. This rare view is now no longer possible, and the character of this whole area has changed for ever. Most of the buildings seen here have now been demolished and the National Computing Centre and the BBC buildings dominate the scene. Buildings off the far right of the picture have been replaced by Manchester Metropolitan University Students' Union.

1946 is the date of this fascinating old photograph, and Victoria Street appears to be full of jay walkers. A crossing with Belisha beacons has been provided, but nobody is using it. All the cars in the picture are pre war, even though it is a year since the end of World War II. Post war prosperity, when most families will own their own car, has yet to come to the ordinary working Mancunian, and in the meantime public transport is the more usual way of getting about. Even so there are a number of interesting, not to say illustrious, vehicles about. One can almost smell the fine leather of the comfortable upholstered interior of the Rolls Royce in the right foreground. The large and sleek upper class saloon ahead is from the other side of the Atlantic, possibly a Chrysler or a Bewick, drawing the eye to its unusual silver grey colour. A Number 16 bus (possibly wearing Salford livery?) is giving way to the horse and cart crossing the intersection; the city still had a large number of working horses during the 1940s. Coming the other way is one of Manchester's last new trams, built in 1929-30 and known as 'Pilcher' cars.

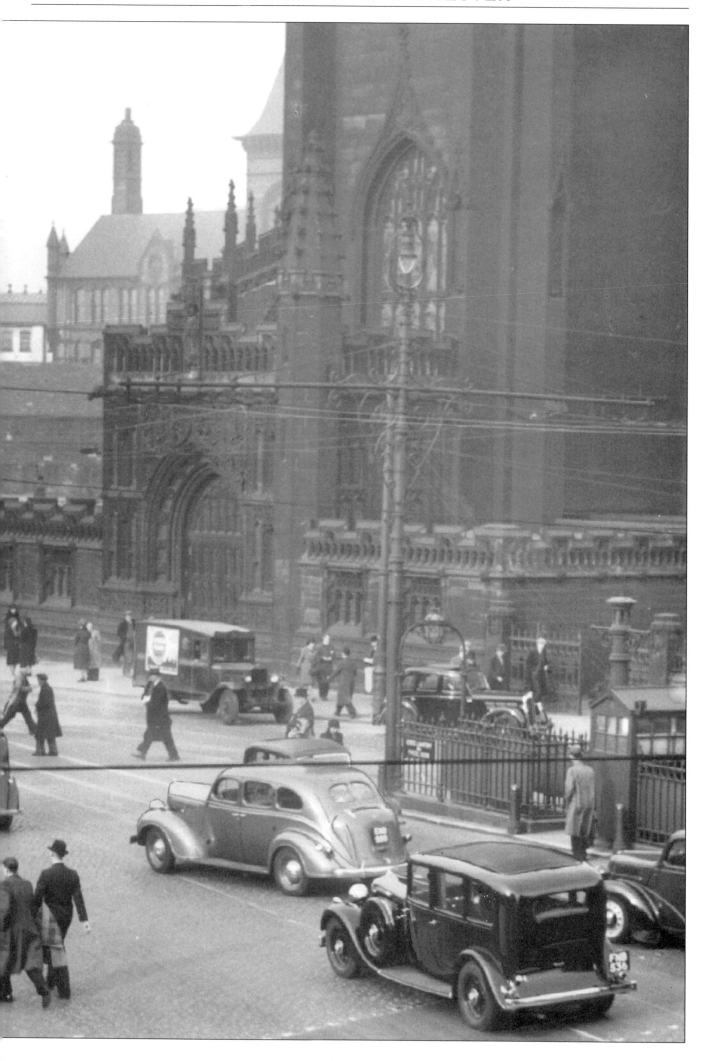

Corporation Street was constructed during the mid 1800s - completed in 1851 - for the sole purpose of relieving congestion in Market Street which had always been a busy route that took traffic out of the city, and even more so on Tuesdays and Thursdays. The buildings at this junction, built during the 1840s and 1850s, did not have much longer to go. The photograph was taken in 1958, and within a few months the whole area was demolished to make room for the next generation of shops, pubs, hotels and offices. Old residents revisiting Market Street would have found themselves in a scene straight out of 'The War of the Worlds', an unrecognisable forest of steel cranes towering above them like H G Wells' alien monsters from Mars. Marks and Spencer now dominates this site, and later on the Arndale Centre would be added, presenting shoppers with a fascinating choice of goods and services. Interestingly, a recommendation was made back in 1906 that the whole area should be pedestrianised; it took another 80 years to bring the vision to fruition.

Manchester Central Library: Local Studies Unit

Manchester Central Library: Local Studies Unit

among the books to the accompaniment of the rather pleasant sound of the Metrolink service that passes through St Peter's Square. The 'square box' ABC building was rushed up at the usual 1960s speed, occupying the site where the Gaiety Theatre had stood a short while before.

Top: Traffic flows smoothly past the soot-grimed but still stately Town Hall in 1958, while parking is allowed in Albert Square. Manchester's first Town Hall stood in King Street, but had only been used for 50 years when it was realised that the premises were becoming far too small. Abel Heywood, who was the city's mayor at the time, campaigned for a new building. The architect Alfred Waterhouse designed the neo Gothic building, and it was chosen by competition in 1868. The site was cleared of its houses, factories and public houses, and the Town Yard, which housed the corporation workshops and fire brigade, was also demolished to make way for the impressive new municipal building. The majestic clock tower dominates Albert Square, and its huge bell was named 'Big Abel' in Mayor Heywood's honour. The Town Hall is as impressive inside as out, and from the vestibule two dramatic ceremonial staircases rise to the lobby of the Great Hall. The mosaic floors, stencilled ceilings and tiled walls were part of Waterhouse's design, and the bee emblem that symbolises Manchester's industry forms part of the beautiful mosaic surfaces, while the cotton flower is worked into the ornate plasterwork, mosaics and even drainpipes.

Above: They say that every picture tells a story, and this one says it all. The year is 1965, and the ABC Weekend Television building stands alongside the Manchester Central Library - styles old and new - and between the two a great gulf is fixed. The Central Library, built on the site of St Peter's Hotel and the Waldorf Restaurant, gives the impression of having been built some hundred years or so ago. But the elegant circular building, the most important addition to the city centre since the building of the Town Hall, was constructed in the early 1930s. It took four years to build and was completed around 1934. The new library was officially opened by King George V and Queen Mary. At the same time the King laid the foundation stone for the new Town Hall extension, neatly potting two birds with one stone. The scene in the photograph is peaceful, but today's library users browse

Enfolded in the embrace of the Town Hall extension, the perfectly circular Manchester Central Library building provides us with an immediate point of reference, while nearby Albert Square provides and open space in the city centre in front of the Town Hall.

The library, completed in 1934, was at that time the largest public library in the country. Two competitions had been held for a design for the library building and the Town Hall extension. Vincent Harris presented a design for both buildings - and both were chosen. The site for the library, which was chosen partly for its proximity to the city centre, was cleared in 1929, and Prime Minister Ramsay McDonald laid the foundation stone on 6th May 1930. King George V declared the library officially open at a ceremony held on 17th July 1934.

The building's elegant rotunda houses the reference section and an impressive entry from St Peter's Square boasts a two storey portico with six elegant columns. The library's collection of works is an impressive one, and in pride of place is a collection of around 30 ancient books which were printed before 1501.

The new city centre is beginning to emerge, as can be seen here in the bottom right corner where the Plaza complex of buildings can just be made out. The Piccadilly redevelopment was the tip of the iceberg; much of the central area around Market Street and Corporation Street was demolished in the 1960s. The Arndale Centre and other modern buildings replaced the old city streets.

At the top of the photograph the Cooperative Insurance Society building rises from the surrounding buildings like a gigantic accusing finger. To the left of the CIS building Cheetham Hill and Corporation Street sweep past Victoria Station, another familiar landmark.

Travellers hurrying for a train rarely have the time to stop and admire their surroundings, but those who do will surely be thankful that the restaurant escaped the redeveloper's drawing board. The Victorians took a lot of trouble to make buildings pleasing to the eye; the ornate 'Refreshment Room' signs are typical of the times, and the original Victorian tiling still covers the walls.

Wartime

Parties of Manchester school children and their teachers board buses on the first stage of their evacuation. The scene was echoed in cities around the country as the nationwide evacuation operation got underway on 1st September 1939. Labelled like packages, and just as impersonally, the children were dispatched to the clean air and safety of the countryside. Four thousand special trains were laid on for the evacuation of school age children, mothers with toddlers and young babies, and the operation went off with clockwork precision. Like soldiers on military exercises none of them were told where they were going.

They arrived at their destination dirty, tired, bewildered and unhappy, and were picked out by householders or assigned to families by officers who had the authority to compel householders to billet a child. Some of the children were contented enough with their new way of life, but others wrote imploring their mothers to come and take them home. A few months later almost half the children had returned to the city. Others also left the danger zones. Civil servants were removed to small and quiet towns; some departments of the BBC moved to Worcester, and the Bank of England relocated to Hampshire.

Manchester Central Library: Local Studies Unit

Left: The first few days of September 1939 were sad days for parents and children alike as Manchester schoolchildren were evacuated from the city. Evacuation to a place of safety was a wise move; in the early days of World War II many children from other parts of the country were even shipped abroad. But even so it must have been heartbreaking for the kiddies who were taken away from their mothers and families. Many had already said goodbye to fathers (some of them for the last time) who had already signed up for military service. It surely took great courage on the part of the parents of these children, to see them packed off to other parts of the country where they would be put into the care of strangers. Some would be fortunate, and be given a place where they would find love and real T.L.C. as part of another family. Others less lucky found themselves lost and lonely, billeted with people who did not like or understand children. The children were given a list of clothing and other items they had to take with them. The all important gas mask came at the top of the list.

Above: This Manchester trolleybus found itself a victim of the 1941 blitz when it was caught while in service by the blast from a high explosive bomb, making its smart red and white livery look decidedly the worse for wear. But Number 1081, brought into service in 1938, was repaired and served Manchester well until it was withdrawn and scrapped in 1951. It was one of a number of buses damaged during the war. Manchester bus operators had a tough time of it during the war. Many of their staff enlisted in the services and women stepped in to replace them where possible. There were other dilemmas to face. Spare parts were like gold dust and were just as elusive. For example, from a total of 225 buses owned by Salford Corporation in 1945 only 169 were usable, and many of those needed urgent maintenance. Yet petrol rationing, coupled with more people commuting to factories, meant that more were using public transport. The blackout too caused problems, and drivers had to learn to 'feel' their way around the city streets, while inside the lights were so dim that the unfortunate conductresses scarcely knew whether they were being given a halfpenny or a shilling.

Above: Mention the word 'hardware' to an average Mancunian before World War II and he would automatically think of Baxendales. Occupying virtually the whole of Miller Street, the hardware stores stocked just about every item imaginable, from agricultural equipment to posts, barrows, bolts and chains. Supplying goods to the trade, Baxendales was a huge concern even at the turn of the 20th Century. By that time they already had an impressive number of employees, with a work force of 1,000, and the company's deliveries were made using an incredible 45 carts and wagons. This photograph was taken after a bombing raid in 1940, when all that was left of Baxendales was a heartbreaking area of smoking rubble and twisted metal. Huge areas of the city were wiped out during the air raid attacks. The wartime raids, coupled with the wholesale demolition work of the 1960s planning department, produced a city centre that is virtually unrecognisable as the pre war Manchester.

Right: 'If the gas rattles sound, put your gas mask on at once, even in bed,' government leaflets instructed the people of Britain during the Second World War. Mustard gas attacks had been feared, and 38 million masks had been distributed as early as 1938. But by 1940 gas fears receded and few people bothered to carry them around any more. When war broke out every effort was made to accustom children to the frightening and claustrophobic gas masks that made parents and friends look like fearsome monsters. This photograph was taken at St Joseph's police premises in Longsight. The little boy on the left looks quite relaxed and confident wearing his mask, though the boy on the right of the picture doesn't seem quite so sure. Children had regular half hour gas mask drills in local community halls. Once they had got used to the strange look of the masks children found the occasions quite exciting. The masks when new were very stiff and tight, and were uncomfortable to wear. After a while they grew comfortable - then along would come an official who would test it, declare it unsafe and issue another quite safe but very uncomfortable mask!

The city prepares for war, and these young girls from Sharston Senior School look remarkably cheerful as they practise their air raid precautions. But then, the reality of war was still a future experience not to be realised until the blitz of 1940-41. The girls' thoughts were perhaps dwelling on happier subjects as they queued up that rainy day, gas masks over their shoulders, to enter the school's air raid shelter. The threat of gas was a very real one; many of these girls' grand-fathers would have suffered from the deadly, all pervasive mustard gas used by the enemy during World War I. So, at least at the outset of World War II, the nation dutifully carried its gas masks everywhere. As the war went on and gas was not used, the masks themselves were as often as not left behind as ladies found the cases just right for carrying lipstick, rouge and a powder compact, and men discovered that a packet of sandwiches would fit nicely into them.

Above: This Leyland Lion bus was given a different and very worthy job to do during World War II. Used by the Air Raid Prevention as a First Aid Post, the vehicle could be quickly moved to the location of any emergency; as quickly, that is, as the state of the roads would allow. Piles of rubble blocking thoroughfares meant that ambulances and public transport faced many detours and could rarely use the same route around the city every day. The nursing staff, often seen as angels in uniform, were on the scene as quickly as possible, however, after an air raid, ready to save lives, bandage injuries and comfort those who had found themselves suddenly homeless. First Aid Posts were set up in many unusual places such as hotels and schools to treat the victims of bomb damage.

Right: Bombs fell indiscriminately during the Second World War, and hospitals and nurses' homes were added to the list of bombed out buildings, often with casualties and sadly, fatalities. The Salford Royal Infirmary was sliced right down the centre by a falling bomb which killed 14 nurses. Some buses were equipped with their own supply of stretchers; perhaps the one in the photograph was one of them? The vehicles would have been used to transfer hospital patients from areas of danger, and the picture shows a small patient being carefully moved from (or into?) the bus via the rear window. Not an ideal exit, but 'where there's a will, there's a way'. The will was certainly there, and the way was obvious. There are records of real heroism by hospital staff; doctors and nurses evacuated a ward full of teenagers when their hospital was hit by high explosive bombs, one of the nurses was herself injured in the raid.

The December blitz of 1940 left little standing in the Shambles and the old Market Place, and a decontamination squad, looking rather sinister in gas masks and protective gear, are cleaning up after the raid. Though many of the surrounding buildings across Fennel Street and the Shambles had gone, the Old Wellington Inn and Sinclair's Oyster Bar, though looking definitely the worse for wear, somehow survived the bombing. The two oldest surviving timber houses in Manchester, their history can be traced back an astounding 600 years to 1328. Down the years they have been altered and added to many times. At one time the Old Wellington was a private house and was owned by John Byrom, the author of the Christmas carol 'Christians Awake'. The rooms above the inn have seen many uses down the centuries; in 1866 a huge pair of spectacles hung outside the upper windows advertising Bowen's 'Practical Opticians and Mathematical Instrument Maker'. By 1900 it was 'Ye Olde Fyshing Tackle Shoppe'. The Old Shambles, which ran between Market Place and Victoria Street, was a popular little street market. In a 1971 preservation scheme the ancient buildings were hydraulically lifted almost five feet and given new foundations.

Manchester Central Library: Local Studies Unit

Above: It was 1939, and Prime Minister Neville Chamberlain had made his announcement to the waiting people of Britain that '...this country is at war with Germany.' Manchester along with the rest of the country rolled up its sleeves and prepared for the inevitable. This war would be different from other wars. This time planes had the ability to fly further and carry a heavier load, and air raids were fully expected. Air raid shelters were obviously going to be needed, and the photograph shows a wooden framework being erected in Albert Square that was to form the basis for the surface shelters. Similar shelters were built on open places across the city, and older Mancunians will remember that they were indeed needed when the expected air raids were made. One became an unexpected labour ward when a woman gave birth to a baby in an air raid shelter in 1940. Other preparations were hastily made. Place names and other identifying marks were obliterated to confuse the enemy about exactly where they were. Notices went up everywhere giving good advice to citizens on a number of issues. 'Keep Mum - she's not so dumb' warned people to take care what kind of information they passed on, as the person they were speaking to could be an enemy.

Right: War had been declared, and every citizen of Britain, young and old, male and female, was called upon to put his or her back into the war effort. Those who did not go into military service of one kind or another worked in factories, dug for victory, gave up their aluminium baths and saucepans, joined organisations and aided in any way they could. These boys from Manchester Grammar School were not going to be left out; they might be too young to fight but while there were sandbags to be filled they were going to do their bit to protect their school building. Thousands of sandbags were used during World War II to protect the city's Victorian heritage and its beautiful civic buildings.

Manchester Grammar School has a long and illustrious history. Founded back in 1515 as the Manchester Free Grammar School, the school has an impressive record of student success, and many of Britain's leading academics and successful businessmen began their student life within its walls. The school abandoned its premises in Long Millgate in 1931, moving out of the city to Fallowfield. The move proved to be fortuitous; a German bomb put paid to the Long Millgate buildings in 1940.

The history of Lancashire Dairies

It was the fertile trading environment of Manchester in the 1840s that gave JJ Kearns the opportunity to create a dairy business that would not only make his fortune, but also satisfy the desperate need for hygienic milk supplies from an undernourished and growing working population.

Like many successful businessmen of the period, James Kearns was not a native of Manchester. In the 1880s he had started a small dairy business in St Helens, Lancashire. The business sold up to ten gallons of milk a day using a method of milk collection and distribution that had remained unchanged for centuries.

JJ Kearns purchased his milk direct from local farmers, a practice that the company has continued down to this day through its dedicated farm supplies.

The milk was sold by the measure from churns strapped to a donkey. As the animal went from house to house it would be preceded by a 'nipper', a small boy who would run or 'nip' to collect orders from customers. It was from these humble

beginnings that today's multi-million pound operation began.

Up until the 1850s, clean milk was almost unknown, and while the traditional methods worked reasonably well in the country, in the city they quickly led to contamination, followed by illness and disease.

The cows themselves were often diseased and kept in filthy cowsheds with the milk stored in unhygienic utensils. The addition of ice was no substitute for the benefits of continuous refrigeration, and as a result, milk usually went sour before it could be consumed.

As the population grew, and the railways made transportation of perishable foodstuffs easier there was a pressing need for a method of milk production that would satisfy demand without causing ill effects. It was not long in coming and by 1894 entrepreneurs were experimenting successfully with 'medicated' milk. It was this atmosphere of innovation that led to the formation of Lancashire Hygienic Dairies in 1898, followed by its official inauguration in 1899.

James Kearns' dairy business grew rapidly, and by the mid 1880s he had two thriving shops on Liverpool Road in St Helens. The shops did well, yet James had

Above: JJ Kearns, founder of Lancashire Dairies.
Left: A street scene of how milk used to be delivered.

set his sights on bigger targets, around 1887 James Kearns 'Milkman' left St Helens to take over the Manchester Pure Milk Company, formerly Matthew Taylors Dairy, in Bradford. The race for market leadership was on.

Now the days of the old-fashioned city dairy were truly numbered and its unhealthy produce was replaced by new, hygienic methods. In 1887 a Mancunian, Anthony Hailwood, exhibited bottles of filtered, medicated milk and in 1894 a method of sterilising was also introduced.

A boom followed, and those companies unable to invest in the new technology were left by the wayside. For a time the strongest and most determined dairy firms - among them James Kearns - consolidated their position as market leaders. But it was not to last. Having broken in to a new and exciting market at the beginning of the decade, by the end of the 1890s the dairy was facing a recession.

As the recession began to bite, it became clear that if they were to survive, the dairymen would have to put aside their differences and join forces. In August 1898 James Kearns and a number of local dairies - including eight of the largest - met at Harrisons Cafe in Stephenson Square, Manchester to discuss the situation. To the chagrin of a number of dairies who quickly dropped out, they decided on amalgamation, and in 1899 Lancashire Hygienic Dairies emerged as a major force in the industry.

The new structure was a combination of James Kearns Limited, The Grange Park Milk Company (with dairies in Bradford, Hulme and Rochdale Road), Harvey & Co and The Creamery, Uttoxeter, a collection point where milk was brought from the farms, checked, weighed and cooled.

The company's headquarters were 65-85 Mulberry Street, Hulme, from where 11 outlets were managed. As managing director, James Kearns took up residence close to the Mulberry Street site in Stretford Road. The company was an immediate success and soon it employed 400 men with over 100 horses. From the Mulberry Street headquarters Lancashire Dairies quickly expanded its business interests. In 1900 the Crystal Ice Company was launched with Bowis and Kearns on the board of directors.

By the time the Victorian era officially ended in 1901, Lancashire Hygienic Dairies was poised to become a leading name in modern, hygienic milk production equipped to meet the very different demands of 20th century consumers. It even sported the latest in transport technology for 1910 - a steam wagon with

solid rubber tyres and a steering wheel shaped like the handle of an old-fashioned mangle. Having acquired cheese factories at Uttoxeter and Sandbach in 1909, the company looked to the future with confidence.

Kearns' knack for positive publicity was clearly evident in his purchase of 'Newstead', a farm at Oakfield Road, Ashton-on-Mersey where he developed a new and exciting concept - the 'model farm'.

The small hygiene-conscious operation, run and managed by the Kearns family, was an outstanding example of what methods of milk production could achieve. The farm was, quite literally, a showpiece where visitors could see cows milked. Passers-by

could purchase free-range eggs and cheese made on the premises, and many years later the farm was also used as a depot.

Throughout the Great War milk production continued unabated, with two doorstep deliveries daily by horse and cart using the traditional churn and can. After guiding the dairy through these difficult years, James Kearns went on to become a well respected figure in the national organisation of the dairy industry.

In an age of unbridled capitalism, where employees were often at the mercy of unscrupulous mill and factory owners, Kearns' concern for the welfare of his charges was outstanding. In fact his fair treatment of workers was to set the tone of the family's treatment of employees for future generations.

Although James Kearns stood firmly against exploitation of his workers, they were, nevertheless expected to adhere to a tough, but fair working regime with roundsmen making two deliveries daily, seven days a week by horse and wagon.

It was not until 1927 that bottled milk began to appear in both pasteurised and sterilised form. Initially the bottles had cardboard tops, later super-seded by wired-on porcelain stoppers with a rubber washer and a message on the bottle that read: "This package is sold as a bottle of milk, not as a measured quantity."

Below: Fresh glass bottling halls 1960s.

Unfortunately, these early milk bottles were much sought after by every dairy in the region and as a result, frequently went missing. So to solve this problem James Kearns set up a bottle bank, Receptacles Recovery Limited, which collected and returned all local milk bottles to their rightful owners.

In 1927, Lancashire Hygienic Dairies recorded a profit of £12,000. By this time it had six shops in East Manchester and six dairies at Sandbach, Bradford, Miles Platting, Oldham, Ashton-Under-Lyne, and Rochdale.

The next few years were to be among the most exciting and challenging in the company's history. Shortly after Harold Kearns' election to the board, the Knowsley Street Dairy was built, coming in to service in 1927. At this time Mulberry Street ceased to function as a processing dairy.

Much of the equipment installed at Knowsley Street was designed by L Jensen, a qualified Danish engineer. Mr Jensen originally worked for Alexander Separator Company using his expertise to help British firms.

James Kearns was so impressed with his expertise that he employed him full-time and he became a director of the company, serving on the board until 1946. During the 1930s acquisitions followed, including the purchase of the Salford Pure Ice Company in 1933, followed by Polar Dairies in 1938.

The stormy years after World War Two were to test the mettle of the company, its employees and its new managing director Harold Kearns. When he became managing director in 1940, Harold inherited his father's upstairs office with its square window overlooking Knowsley Street with its leather swivel chair, steel filing cabinets, tall dial phone and a table that served for a desk.

The establishment of the Milk Marketing Board in 1933 had paved the way to growth for Lancashire Dairies. Prior to its formation, milk supply had been a contentious issue between the dairy and the farmers who always believed they could get a better price for their milk.

During the war however, normal trading conditions were virtually suspended. Milk production and even the dairy's customers, were controlled by the Ministry of Food under Lord Walton. Price regulation and rationing using milk tokens were also introduced. Even so, in 1940, the company managed to secure the first ever order to export fresh milk to France.

Under the new food and fuel regime, milk was allocated a maximum and minimum retail price. The Ministry allocated a set number of streets to each dairy, and the business customers were made to register for supplies.

Just prior to Christmas 1940 the people of Manchester experienced the terrors of the Blitz. Although London and Coventry bore the brunt of the assault, the bombs and incendiaries of the Luftwaffe also set many parts of Manchester ablaze from Portland Street to Victoria Station.

Fortunately Knowsley Street never experienced a direct hit. Incendiary bombs posed a major threat, but thanks to the vigilance of the company's employees on firewatch duties, major fires were avoided. One worker, Harold Sweetman, is reported to have seen an incendiary bomb on the roof of Knowsley Street and to have kicked it to the ground before it ignited!

In 1954 the company acquired Handforth's Dairy, a busy depot serving the Salford, and Eccles areas. In 1957 the company made a massive investment in its Knowsley Street operation, installing the largest milk pasteurising unit in the north west of England.

By now, milk in bottles was becoming old-fashioned and the Dairy was already busy experimenting with alternatives. In 1960, in conjunction with Express Dairies, the company launched the then revolutionary Tetrahedron-shaped paper milk carton from Tetra Pak, an event that marked the beginning of the end for milk bottles.

In 1963 Lancashire Hygienic Dairies acquired Frosts of Crumpsall, and in 1965 Mulberry Street was demolished to make way for Manchester's urban redevelopment programme. At that time the company consolidated its headquarters at Knowsley Street and in 1968 became only the second UK dairy to sell milk in plastic bottles.

In the years that followed, the company got down to the serious business of establishing itself as the region's largest and most advanced dairy operation. In 1975, the Board of Lancashire Dairies comprised of JH Kearns' two sons, Peter and Patrick, joint managing directors, and Mr Ellis Arter. These experienced men were to oversee a period of major growth and expansion into new markets that the company's founder would have found hard to foresee.

During the 1970s the company foresaw a number of changes in patterns of milk consumption and took steps to ensure that Lancashire Dairies invested to cater for emerging market demands.

Lancashire Dairies was the first British dairy operation to supply sterilised milk to shops and supermarkets in non-returnable plastic bottles. In 1975 the Knowsley Street premises were extended to accommodate production with a massive £350,000 investment in modern processing and bottling plant.

In no time, new markets for Ultra-Life, later known as 'SuperLife', began to open up both at home and abroad. Its long shelf life - up to six months in a tropical climate proved irresistible to buyers from countries where high temperatures had previously made non-refrigerated milk storage impossible. Over the years, SuperLife has also become available in a wide variety of mouth watering flavours, including strawberry, chocolate, blackcurrant, banana and mango.

In 1985, 5,000 gallons of SuperLife was being shipped by container from Felixstowe to destinations around the globe, from Singapore to Kuala Lumpur, Malaysia, the West Indies, and Egypt. In this year the company moved its head office to Derby Street, this coincided with the beginning of UHT production.

In 1995 came Shake Rattle and Roll, one of the UK's first long-life thick and creamy milk shakes which was launched in chocolate, banana and strawberry flavours in a unique bottle design.

In its one hundred years of existence, Lancashire Dairies has grown from a one-man operation producing 10 gallons a day, to a £100 million turnover company with national brands with in excess of 600 employees processing a massive 200 million litres of milk annually for consumption by thousands of homes the world over.

When James Kearns set off for Manchester all those years ago he could never have foreseen the outcome of his vision to create hygienic milk for the working people of Manchester. Yet as Lancashire Dairies faces the new millennium one thing is certain, the journey JJ Kearns set out on all those years ago has hardly begun.

Below: *Sterilisation Plant, Lancashire Dairies.*
Facing Page: *Harold Kearns, director.*

Events & occasions

Below: The Union Jack has been painted upside down, but who cares - the war is over! It's party time for every family in the street; neighbours and friends join together and sing a victory song (The National Anthem? 'Rule Britannia'?); bunting is strung from house to house across the street and patriotic flags stir gently in the breeze. Can we detect the Russian hammer and sickle flying there alongside the stars and stripes of America? All were Britain's gallant allies during World War II. When peace was declared after six long years of war this wonderful scene of joy was repeated in every street across the length and breadth of Great Britain. It was Britain's new Prime Minister, Clement Attlee, who brought the nation down from its euphoria with a resounding bump. He gave the country a serious warning that although Britain was once more at peace, there was no likelihood of prosperity for the country in the immediate future. Across the world, countries were decimated by war, and there were worldwide food shortages. It would be several more years before people could stop using tinned dried eggs or shop for clothes without counting how many coupons they had.

Right: The war was over, and the citizens of Manchester were tired of bombs, gas masks, the blackout and all the other privations of wartime Britain. Out came the flags and the bunting and the photograph of good old 'Winnie', as Winston Churchill was affectionately known. Dust was blown off the accordion, and this entire community went wild with joy when the news that everybody was waiting for was announced. It was good to be alive, and along with the rest of Britain they found the energy to let their hair down and organise a knees-up. There was to be no immediate let up in the food rationing that Britain had grown used to during the war, however. In fact a year later in 1946 bread went on ration, though the first bananas that had been seen since before the war arrived from the West Indies. Children born during the war had never seen a banana before, and had no idea that they had to peel off the skin before they could eat them. For a good while to come saccharin tablets still went into tea cups in place of sugar, and (reputedly) whale oil margarine was still spread on the nation's bread.

When her Majesty the Queen was crowned in Westminster Abbey on 2nd June 1953, the nation relaxed for the first time since the end of World War II in 1945. The event was an ideal opportunity for Mancunians to state their patriotism, and an excuse for a city wide party.
A few of them would perhaps get to watch the crowning of the Queen in Westminster Abbey on television - the first time a Coronation has ever been filmed. Though Britain had a television service as early as 1936, few people could afford to buy the expensive sets. By the 1950s they were beginning to get cheaper, and the Queen's Coronation presented many families with the ideal reason to buy or rent a TV set. Those who did not simply crowded into the parlours of more fortunate neighbours to watch the event! Television took off in a big way during the 1950s and sadly spelled the end of many of the local cinemas that were dotted around the city. Many fought valiantly on as bingo clubs and some, such as the huge bingo club out at Belle Vue, remained popular.

Left: The people of Manchester have always loved a good celebration, and Coronation fever hit Manchester in 1953 when Elizabeth I was crowned Queen. This fascinating old photograph gives us some idea of what the town must have looked like on that memorable occasion when a rather different Albert Square from the one we know today was decked out in banners. A Union flag snaps in the breeze from the Town Hall flagstaff, and Prince Albert, Queen Victoria's consort, gazes impassively from his ornate memorial at the smart decorations that mark the accession of another queen to the throne.

This kind of scene was repeated in many homes and communities around the city. Colourful bunting was strung across the streets and patriotic Mancunians flew flags from every available window. The initials 'E II R' faced the street from parlour windows and the tops of lamp posts as the town geared up for its wild party. Coronation Day itself was dull and rather damp, but nothing could dampen Manchester's party spirit. Some street parties were hastily rearranged and were held in Sunday Schools and local school rooms, while others went ahead as planned in spite of the weather.

Above: A scene that was repeated in many towns and cities across Britain - a walkout by bus drivers and conductors. The long queue of people on the pavement, probably at the top end of Market Street near Paulden's, are presumably waiting for a bus, and however sympathetic they are with the demands made by the busmen, that doesn't solve their immediate problem, which is to get home from work as quickly as possible. How many of these would-be passengers ended up walking several miles home that evening back in 1955? The exact reason for the walk out is not clear, but the strike would most likely have been about pay, the number of hours they were expected to put in, or possibly about the conditions of work. It was not until the Thatcher Government of the 1980s that various measures were introduced as an attempt to curb trade union power to strike. An Act was passed in 1984 that made a secret ballot of members obligatory before a strike.

Sporting life

Left: September 1959, and hundreds of United fans crowd the turnstiles. 1959 was a memorable year; the club was still reeling from the effects of the Munich air disaster that took the lives of seven of the 'Busby Babes' on 6th February 1958 and left Matt Busby in a critical condition. Chairman Harold Hardman gave his promise that the club would go on. Many regarded it as an impossible task, as the Babes had featured some of the best players of their generation, but Assistant Manager Jimmy Murphy determinedly set about rebuilding the team. He promoted junior and reserve team players and made emergency signings and the team completed that season's fixtures. The United that emerged possessed its own unique flavour. Wilf McGuinness, Warren Bradley and Albert Quixall came into the side and a 3-1 win over Leicester City secured the FA Cup in the 62/63 season. But the best was yet to be; Bobby Charlton captained United to European Cup victory in May 1968, a thrilling 4-1 win over Benifica at Wembley making United the first English club to win the European Cup. That same year Matt Busby's services to football were acknowledged when he received a knighthood from the Queen.

Below: Larry Gains was one of the boxers seen here sparring to music. The name of his partner has been forgotten, as has the reason why this event was staged. Whatever the reason behind it, this must have been an interesting and very tuneful occasion. The photograph actually dates back to 1938, though at first glance it appears to be much more recent. We tend to think that guitars originated with the pop music that took off a few decades ago, but the acoustic guitar was actually popular during medieval times. The guitar played a supporting harmony role in jazz and dance bands during the 1920s. The solid bodied electric guitar was developed in the 1950s. The polo neck sweaters worn in the photograph are trendy even today, and also send out the wrong signals. The real clues to the age of the photo can be found in the short hairstyles and the pleated style of the jackets worn by the musicians in the foreground, and in the rather formal dress of the boxers, which is certainly not the usual type of 90s sporting gear!

Bottom: Kings Hall, Belle Vue, was a focal point for wrestling and boxing enthusiasts. Though the sport was discontinued for the duration of World War II, it quickly re-established its reputation during the post war years. This atmospheric photograph, which dates from around 1960, gives us a taste of what it must have been like in its heyday, when vast crowds converged upon the hall, rooting for well known wrestlers such as Jack Pye, who emerged as one of Belle Vue's major sporting personalities between the 1940s and 1960s. Surprisingly for the time before women's lib had burnt many of its bras, the promotion of wrestling at Belle Vue was undertaken by Kathleen Look. Miss Look was Britain's only woman promoter; her highly professional handling of the job brought credit to the sport.

Kings Hall, one of the largest outside London, was the venue for many types of event. An annual Christmas Circus was staged there (though the ceiling was too low for high wire acts). During the 1960s it became the largest Bingo hall in the country, and the popular game was played at Kings Hall twice every week. Audiences rioted, however, during a Rolling Stones concert on 8th August 1964.

Right: A glimpse back in time to one of the many turnstiles that ushered spectators into the massive Old Trafford Cricket Ground - possibly the Warwick Road entrance. The history of the ground goes back a very long way; the very first county match was played there as long ago as 1865, when Lancashire and Middlesex battled it out between 20th and 22nd June. Naturally, Lancashire emerged as the winner by 62 runs. The ground suffered a number of battles of a very different nature during World War II. Much of the site was taken over by the Royal Engineers, and it was also used as a war transit camp. The Ministry of Supply used the Old Trafford ground for storage. Nazi air raids caused havoc at Old Trafford during the Blitz; many of the buildings were damaged or destroyed during bombing raids, and an enormous crater was left in the outfield. Life slowly returned to normal during the post war years; a match that lingers in the memory was in 1956, when Laker took 19 Aussie wickets in 1956. For lovers of cricketing trivia, the highest score at Old Trafford was made in 1911, when Lancashire scored 676 for 7 against Hampshire.

Below: The year is 1950 and Manchester City goalkeeper Bert Trautman is mobbed by an eager crowd of young fans, all clamouring for his autograph. Trautman played a memorable game six years later when City won the FA Cup, beating Birmingham City 3-1. During the game Trautman sustained injuries that proved more serious than he had realised - he had played on to the end of the game with a broken neck! Lucky to be walking about, Bert Trautman recovered from the injury and continued his involvement with City. After World War II City gained promotion to the First Division, and Trautman became one of the club's key players. The Blues won the FA cup for the first time back in 1904, beating Bolton Wanderers 1-0. They finished runners up in the League, scoring more goals than any other club.1969-70 were great years. Manchester City celebrated an FA Cup win in 69 after beating Leicester City 1-0. In 1970 City achieved a superb double, winning the League Cup at Wembley by beating West Brom 2-1 in extra time. They went on to win the European Cup - Winners Cup later the same season, beating Poland's Gornik Zabrze by 2-1 in Vienna.

Above: A tense moment in the game between Manchester United FC and Tottenham in 1951 as Jack Rowley runs in to take the ball. Note the thousands upon thousands of fans overflowing the terraces in this dramatic photograph, taken before the rise in popularity of TV sets. Today the ground seats 55,000, but scenes such as this are not seen so often today. TV coverage affected attendance, and while the atmosphere of the game is lost, many still opt to watch the match in the comfort of their own homes with a few cans of the right stuff. United moved to Old Trafford in 1910, and a crowd of 45,000 watched the club play their first match against Liverpool. The Second World War proved a difficult time for Man United; soon after war was declared the game was suspended, and Old Trafford was bombed twice in the space of a few months. In the first season of play after the war, new manager Matt Busby began creating history with his 'Busby Babes'. On his death in 1994, thousands of fans left scarves as a tribute to the great man; the bales of scarves were sealed inside a hollow bronze statue of Sir Matt Busby.

Above right: A splendid kick by Bobby Charlton sends the ball towards City's net in a game between Manchester United and Manchester City in 1967. That was the never to be forgotten year when United lifted the European Cup at Wembley. Bobby Charlton gave United the

lead, only for Graca of Benifica to equalise. The game went into extra time and George Best quickly restored the Red Devils' lead. Another goal from Charlton and a header from birthday boy Brian Kidd (nineteen years old that day), secured the 4-1 victory. Bobby Charlton was only 17 years old when he signed for United in 1955, and quickly proved his worth. He went on to carve out an illustrious career in the game, playing in three Championship winning sides, winning an FA Cup Winners medal and captaining United to European Cup victory. He was elected Footballer of the Year and European Player of the Year in 1966. In the summer of 1994 Bobby Charlton was recognised for his services to the game and became Sir Bobby Charlton OBE.

Bird's eye view

The 36 mile long Manchester Ship Canal heads in the direction of Old Trafford before making a dramatic sweep to the left, past Pomona Docks and out towards Ordsall. Timber was for many years a major import to the bustling Salford Docks. Vessels headed up the Canal bringing china clay from Cornwall, Egyptian cotton from Alexandria and Middle East produce from ports in the Mediterranean. When war broke out in 1939, the Manchester Liners fleet had a total of 10 vessels. The merchant ships were repainted in camouflage livery, and carried no names or markings. Three of them were lost during the war; the third vessel, 'Manchester City' was requisitioned by the Admiralty. Among the many ships torpedoed at sea, 'Manchester City' managed to survive and remained in service until 1964. Air raids during 1940-41 targeted the docks and the many factories in the surrounding area, but the Company succeeded in keeping the waterway open.Peace eventually returned; operations at the docks got back to normal and vessels resumed their smart pre war livery, slowly reverting to their peace time activities. The canal was very busy during the 1950s. Between 1954 and 1974 the annual traffic using the docks totalled 16,000,000 tons.

Above: *A dramatic photograph of Salford Docks, giving us a closer view of the rows of vast warehouses that line the dockside, and the number of large vessels discharging cargo in No 9 Dock. A large ship is docked at Trafford Wharf in the foreground. The Manchester Ship Canal was built towards the end of the 19th Century as an answer to high railway charges and rocketing charges at Liverpool Docks. The building started in November 1887, and Queen Victoria herself declared the Manchester Ship Canal open in May, 1894. Immediately trade took off, justifying the £15 million it cost to build. 925,000 tons of traffic entered the Port of Manchester in its first year. Less than a hundred years later the heyday of the Manchester Ship Canal was over, and grain elevators were demolished and rail tracks torn up. In the 1990s, however, a new lease of life was given to Salford Docks with the Salford Quay Development. The old docks were divided into water parks, a marina was built and No 7 Dock was stocked with fish for anglers. With an eye to the leisure industry, hotels and leisure facilities were built and new office blocks and houses were constructed.*

Right: *This view of Salford Docks, captured in March 1972, gives us some idea of the immensity of what things must have been like in the heyday of the Manchester Ship Canal. The docks, though largely in Salford and Stretford, were nevertheless a Manchester enterprise and the port was a thriving centre for Britain's exports. Even the high viewpoint cannot dwarf the enormous gantries at Number 2 Dock at the bottom left of the photograph. How many men spent their entire working life in this truly amazing environment, like Gulliver in the land of Lilliput? A solitary vessel is docked at No 8 Pier in the centre of the picture, and opposite, a number of vessels along Trafford Wharf. Trafford Wharf Road, the straight road on the right, takes traffic away towards the swing bridge in the distance. By the 1970s the number of large ships using the docks had begun to decline, a situation accelerated by repeated strikes over the last couple of decades. Strikes staged by dock workers in the 1950s hit the Company hard and a 47 day strike in 1966 severely disrupted programme development. By 1970 customers began to take their cargoes elsewhere; signalling the beginning of the end.*

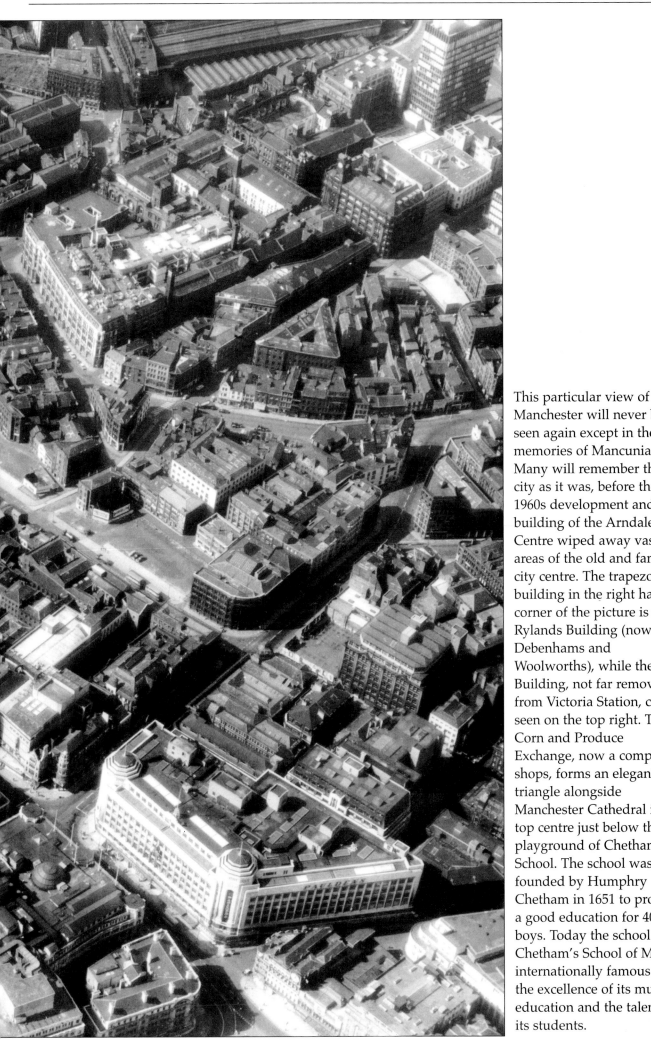

This particular view of Manchester will never be seen again except in the memories of Mancunians. Many will remember the city as it was, before the 1960s development and the building of the Arndale Centre wiped away vast areas of the old and familiar city centre. The trapezoidal building in the right hand corner of the picture is the Rylands Building (now Debenhams and Woolworths), while the CIS Building, not far removed from Victoria Station, can be seen on the top right. The Corn and Produce Exchange, now a complex of shops, forms an elegant triangle alongside Manchester Cathedral in the top centre just below the playground of Chethams School. The school was founded by Humphry Chetham in 1651 to provide a good education for 40 poor boys. Today the school is Chetham's School of Music, internationally famous for the excellence of its musical education and the talent of its students.

One must be thankful that whatever other sweeping changes have been made to the city of Manchester, Piccadilly gardens (centre picture) still survive today, having continued to provide a haven of peace in the hustle and bustle of the city since they were created in 1908. The 19th Century saw many fine Victorian buildings erected, and the horrors of war during the early 1940s saw many of them wiped away again along with 30,000 homes. Many people lost their lives during those years, and when all is said and done, people matter more than streets and buildings. The post war years were times of change and progression. Many of the changes were not wanted by the majority of Mancunians; their familiar surroundings were taken away and replaced by soaring constructions of glass and stone and concrete. Yet we have learned to live with them, appreciate them, and in some cases, dare we say, develop a fondness for them. Looking back down the years many of the changes made to the city in the 1960s and 70s have offered the average person in the street a better and more prosperous way of life than that of their grandparents.

Below: Manchester speedway racing originally took place at the Greyhound Stadium, but as the sport gained in popularity it was clear that it would need a purpose built stadium. The Belle Vue speedway stadium was opened in March 1929, eight years before this photograph was taken in August of 1937. Originally termed 'dirt track racing', speedway originated in Australia. E O Spence was speedway manager at Belle Vue until 1941. Early in World War II he moved on to become Managing Director of the Belle Vue Company until he died in 1947. Speedway was interrupted by the war for a while, then continued, and the highly successful home team, The Aces, owed much to the skill of riders such as Eric Langton and Frank (Red Devil) Varey. A popular innovation was added to the meetings during 1954 in the form of 'Johnnie's Marching Girls', a British version of the American cheerleader squad. Thirteen young and pretty girls clad in red and white costumes would enliven each speedway meeting with performances at regular intervals. The speedway stadium was often put to alternative uses. Tattoos were held there soon after the stadium was completed, and the spectacular Lancashire Cotton Pageant was staged there in 1932.

Right: The stadium at Belle Vue was opened on 23 March 1929, and was a mecca for devotees of speedway in general and the Aces in particular. Purpose built for the sport, the stadium nevertheless lent itself to a variety of other uses. Stock car racing was introduced in June 1954 with considerable success. Nine meetings were held every year until Belle Vue Stadium closed down. The last stock car event was held on 14th November 1987, and the stadium was demolished only weeks later to make way for a British Car Auction Group development.

Belle Vue's popularity as an all round family entertainment soared during the post war years. But even as early as 1951 attendances were beginning to slip, and only four years later the management were in real trouble. Sir Leslie Joseph and Charles Forte stepped in with a rescue package and transformed the pleasure grounds, giving Belle Vue the new lease of life it so badly needed. Entrances were remodelled, a lot of refurbishments were done, and a large Bingo club was opened in Kings Hall, which proved to be very popular. By 1962 attendances were up again once more.

Left: The Arndale Centre with its convenient concentration of under cover shopping which was completed in the mid 1970s has replaced many of the buildings viewed here in this 1963 photograph. The long buildings of the Exchange Station, connected to Victoria Station by what was reputed to be the longest platform in the world, can be seen at the top of the photograph. The station was never fully restored after being badly damaged in the 1940s bombing raids, and the Exchange was closed in 1969, the site providing the city with another car park.

Just across the Irwell. the Cathedral can just be picked out. The very ancient Cathedral dates right back to 1422, and like all old buildings it was improved and added to over the years. Five hundred years of history were almost lost during a bombing raid in World War II; the damage caused was so severe that it was believed that the lovely old church was beyond repair. It was restored, however, and fifty years on the Cathedral still offers hope to the Christians of Manchester. The triangular site nearby once housed the soot-blackened Victoria buildings. Destroyed by bombs in 1940, the site was cleared and transformed into pleasant public gardens.

Below: The massive arched roof of Manchester Central Station, the city's last railway terminus, draws the eye immediately to its almost central position in this dramatic photograph. Built for three companies which formed the Cheshire Lines Committee, the huge iron and glass structure was second only in size to that of St Pancras Station in London. The Beeching Act of 1969 closed the station, which gradually deteriorated over the next few years. Eventually Greater Manchester County Council acquired the old station building and converted it to the G-Mex Centre. The conversion has fortunately not wiped away the exhibition centre's origins; the domed roof and the lovely old clock set amid the glass panes still proclaim its Victorian origins. The nearby goods station also closed down, and the railway bridge that crossed Deansgate was demolished. Following the line of buildings upwards from the station is the huge YMCA building on the corner of Mount Street, whose red terracotta cannot be detected from this height. This symbol of Victorian respectability housed a 60 foot long swimming pool, a running track, a gymnasium and a hall with seating for 900 people. The buildings at the bottom right of the photograph are those of the Gas Works in Cambridge Street.

Manchester city centre as it was a couple of decades ago, spread out below like a three dimensional map. Slightly off centre towards the top of the photograph we can pick out the walkways and flower beds of Piccadilly Gardens, the bus station and the Plaza Suite site. The Town Hall and its extension and the dramatic Public Library dominate the scene; the YMCA is the almost triangular building next to the library. In Albert Square the Prince Consort's memorial can be seen, taking pride of place in the open square in front of the civic buildings. Statues of other respected Victorian reformers and politicians Bishop James Fraser, John Bright, W E Gladstone and Oliver Heywood remind passing Mancunians of their heritage. Thomas Worthington designed the tall Gothic canopy that shelters Prince Albert's statue, developing his design from a sketch he had made of a chapel during a visit to Pisa nearly 20 years earlier. Victoria's Consort, the German Prince Albert, was at first looked on with suspicion by most Britons. Although rather straight-laced for British taste, the Prince established a reputation as a man of wisdom and eventually gained the respect of the British public.

Belle Vue Lake and Firework Island, pictured here in 1949. Spectacular annual firework displays were held at Belle Vue for many years. This took the form of a play with actors, usually featuring a battle of some kind or perhaps having a piratical theme. Whatever the theme the audience could always expect lots of thrilling bangs, crashes and flashes. The 1926 show was 'The Reign of Terror'; in 1936 the ballet 'San Sebastian 1836' was staged. Firework displays, discontinued during World War II, were reintroduced in 1947, though without actors. In 1954 a move was made to reintroduce the old battlepieces, and 'The Storming of Quebec' was staged. The show, which had synchronised sound tracks and 250 actors, took many months of rehearsal to bring it to perfection, and the actual performances lasted for thirty minutes. The show was planned to last for eight weeks but in the end had to be extended in response to popular demand. 'The Relief of Lucknow' was performed in 1955 and 'Robin Hood' the following year. But audiences were falling as the public demanded more sophisticated effects. After the 1956 performance only ordinary firework displays were put on, and even these were discontinued in 1969.

At leisure

Bottom: Piccadilly Gardens had been a favourite spot with Mancunians since the garden was created after the demolition in 1908 of Manchester Royal Infirmary, which had stood for many years on the site. The beautiful sunken garden provided a relaxing place to rest tired feet after a hard morning's shopping, or to sit and eat a packed lunch away from the office on a sunny day. During the war years however, the gardens provided a refuge of a very different kind. When war was declared the flower beds and lawns surrounding the sunken garden were dug up, and surface air raid shelters were built for those caught in the city centre during a raid. Communal shelters were never very popular, and people who had gardens to build them in much preferred to use their own Anderson shelter when-

ever possible. Anywhere underground was considered safer than surface shelters, and many people had their cellars especially strengthened. Others huddled under the stairs or in coal holes. The photograph shows a number of the air raid shelters at the far side of the ornamental gardens.

Below left: August 1945, and the war in Europe had ended three months earlier. These Mancunians enjoying the peace in Piccadilly Gardens did not know it, but Britain and her allies were just one week away from victory over Japan. The scars that the city suffered from enemy bombing would be there for some time to come, as would the personal inner scars that none could see. Along with the rest of the country the citizens of Manchester had

prided themselves on 'business as usual' during the air raids that had devastated the homes and businesses of the city. They had gone through evacuation of their children, hung blackout curtains at their windows, dug up their gardens for Anderson shelters, replaced roses with potatoes and sweet peas with runner beans, manned ARP posts and first aid posts - and mourned their own losses. Their peace had been hard won, and they deserved it. Perhaps some of those sitting around the peaceful Piccadilly gardens on that August day were reflecting on what kind of life the future would bring to them and to their children.

Above: Alan Bates and June Ritchie, a new find, were the lovers in the 'X' rated movie 'A Kind of Loving' which was showing at the ABC Cinema in 1962. Thora Hird played June Ritchie's domineering middle class mother, who believed that Bates's character was not good enough for her daughter. The actor Alan Bates is remembered by most film buffs for his nude scenes in D H Lawrence's 'Women in Love', in which he starred with Glenda Jackson and Oliver Reed. The modern and popular Deansgate cinema opposite the Barton Arcade survived television and was a focal point for city centre cinema-goers until the 1980s - 90s. Sadly, falling audiences, possibly hastened on by the growing trend for renting films on video, brought about its demise. The building's use changed, and it is currently a popular pub, providing Mancunians with a night out and the liquid refreshment they need.

Inset: Mancunians have always enjoyed a night out as much as anyone else, and the city has long offered them a bewildering choice of cinemas, pubs, clubs, dance halls and theatres. Remember the Gaumont? This dramatic photograph of the ultra-modern Gaumont Cinema in Oxford Street was taken in 1935, when the film 'The Rage of Paris', starring Douglas Fairbanks Junior, was being screened. Back in 1904 the old Hippodrome was providing enter-tainment for the citizens of Manchester on the same site. The Hippodrome ended its days around 1934/35, becoming the Ardwick Hippodrome. It was later redeveloped as a cinema and became the Gaumont. The building's yellow tiles were a fashionable feature of the day. The chocolate shop is nicely placed between the Gaumont and the New Oxford Theatre, and must have been very well patro-nised. The Gaumont came to a sad end, as many did across the city when the growing popularity of television badly affected cinema audiences, and the whole block was demolished. By the late 1990s the site was used as a car park; who knows what its future holds?

The Gaumont Cinema in Chorlton-cum-Hardy has a chequered history. Opening as the Majestic it then became the Savoy, next the Gaumont, then the ABC - and is currently an undertaker's parlour. The children in this 1958 photograph have just been to the Saturday matinee. These children's shows were great value for money, and for just a few coppers they could see one of the popular cartoons, a couple of feature films, and often a 'cliffhanger' serial that left the heroine tied to the railway line for a nail-biting week until next Saturday. In the meantime they would hope against hope that nothing would prevent them from finding out what happened to the luckless female - though deep down they knew full well that some super-hero would come along and rescue her in the nick of time. Between the films, exciting trailers of forthcoming films would entice them back time and again. The whole programme was, of course, punctuated by cheers and jeers, flying bits of rubbish, the popping of bubble gum, the 'oohs' of excitement, and the shouts of 'Put a penny in!' that harassed the long suffering projectionist when the film broke, as frequently happened. All very thrilling stuff.

Manchester Central Library: Local Studies Unit

Belle Vue's elephants acted as a magnet for the kiddies, and for years hundreds of intrepid youngsters queued up to take a ride high above the ground on the swaying wooden seats carried on each side of the magnificent animal. The exotically dressed figure seen in the photograph with the elephant was Phil Fernandez; an unlikely name for the Malayan keeper who joined the team at Belle Vue's zoo as early as 1921, bringing with him his elephant Lil. It is quite possible that the elephant in this photograph is Lil herself. Fernandez was a familiar sight around the complex, always in the oriental robes that gave the attraction an aura of Eastern mystery. Lil was not the only elephant at Belle Vue; another was called Mary, and Annie was purchased from Sangers Circus in 1941 at a cost of 50 guineas. (Readers too young to remember guineas might like to know that a guinea was worth one pound and one shilling - £1.5p in today's currency.) Fernandez remained at Belle Vue and was in charge of the elephant rides until his own death in 1956. By that time a new children's zoo had been introduced at a cost of £15,000.

Left: You don't see a string of elephants parading around the streets of Manchester every day, and here the camera has captured the eager crowd of onlookers who gathered to watch the unusual sight. A circus was introduced to Belle Vue pleasure grounds as early as 1929, and was put in the sole charge of the well known Blackpool Tower ringmaster George Lockhart. The circus was one of the few Belle Vue attractions to be kept going (albeit with great difficulty) during World War II, though in the blitz of 1940 and 1941 only afternoon performances were possible. Most of the staff were, of course, fighting for king and country, and George Lockhart carried on single handedly all through the war. Lockhart, described as the 'Prince of Ringmasters', was a very able linguist, and his charm and charisma gave him instant rapport with audiences. His position as ringmaster gave him authority over all the acts and carried great responsibility. Lockhart went on working long after most men of his years had opted for a pipe and slippers, eventually retiring in 1972 at the amazing age of 90! His name lives on as a street name on one of Manchester's Wimpey housing estates.

Below: The year is 1946, and vast crowds descend on Belle Vue fun fair for a day's relaxation. The war had been over for a year, but there are still a few people among the crowd wearing uniform. Belle Vue had many popular rides such as the miniature railway, the Bug and the Bobs - but at that time you might have queued for up to three quarters of an hour for a turn on the Caterpillar. That particular ride was so popular, in fact, that for a while a second Caterpillar had to be installed to relieve the queues! The original ride was not demolished until the early 1970s. The scenic railway, a popular ride that dominated Belle Vue fun fair, can just be made out in the background of the picture. The Bobs, a hair raising switchback experience, took courage and a strong stomach. The Bobs was also demolished around 1971. Victory in World War II had not long been won, and interestingly 'Over the Falls', another Belle Vue ride, had a large sculpture of leader Joseph Stalin mounted over the entrance to the ride as a tribute our valiant Russian allies and the part Russia played in the war.

The date given for this photograph is 1957, though the costumes worn by people in the crowd at Belle Vue fun fair would appear to be from a decade earlier. The Caterpillar remained a popular ride for many years and was a rather more thrilling experience than the Ocean Wave which was one of Belle Vue's first amusements, and was popular during the 1920s. Tame by today's hair raising standards, the Ocean Wave was built after the 'Sea on Land' type of ride that was common in Victorian times. The bridge of a ship was created on a large roundabout amid scenery that was painted to look like storm dashed waves. As an internal machine rotated the roundabout, small boats set among the waves rose and fell to the accompaniment of squeals of delight from the boats' occupants. Other amusements that were popular during the very early years of Belle Vue was its fledgling zoo. Back then people had little experience of the wider world and its fauna, and six policemen had to control the huge crowds who mobbed the amusement park to see an orang utan billed as the 'Wild Man of Borneo'.

Above: During the 1940s and 50s a fun day out meant a day at Belle Vue, not just for Mancunians but for families across the North of England, and millions went through the turnstiles of the pleasure park when Belle Vue was at its peak of popularity. Many readers will remember the little pleasure steamer 'Little Eastern'; the whole family would enjoy the sail around the large boating lake, and the pleasure of the passengers in the photograph is reflected in their wide smiles. The motor boat was no doubt popular with dads who might otherwise have found themselves expending muscle power with a pair of oars.

Right: The park's popularity began to wane in the 1960s, and in 1977, one stage at a time, the attraction shut down. The area was eventually developed as private housing and commercial property. Promoted by Len Myatt, who still lives in the area, the 50-mile cycle race was a regular event held in Heaton Park, Manchester. Permission to hold the race would of course have to be applied for and granted by the Corporation. Perhaps four or five times a year competitors would gather in the Park, and 50 or 60 riders would power around the circuit (which was roughly one and a half miles), completing 40 or so laps. Riders Bill Bradley, Geoff Broadbent and Derek Clark often finished as winners and were well known in their day. The photograph was taken in 1950. Was this before or after the race, one wonders. The riders look quite relaxed, making it more probable that the race is over, the winner declared and it is time to adjourn to the pub to dissect the race, decide where improvements could be made in their performance and applaud the snap judgments that had swung the race their way. Students' track events were often held in Fallowfield Stadium, Stretford. Reg Harris, a regular winner, was amateur sprint champion on the 100m track. Harris eventually took over the running of Manchester Athletic Club.

Manchester Central Library: Local Studies Unit

Above: A determined group of young athletes steps out with confident stride - each one a competitor in the All England Athletics Championships, and each one hoping for victory for himself and for his team. Athletics events were often staged at Belle Vue Stadium, and this particular championship took place in 1955. Belle Vue had the facilities to hold not only large sporting events, but other types of meetings were also staged there such as pageants, flower shows, Mothers' Union rallies and Brass Band Championships. The skills of running, jumping, throwing, wrestling and boxing go back a surprisingly long way, and the sports were all practised in Ancient Greece. In Britain

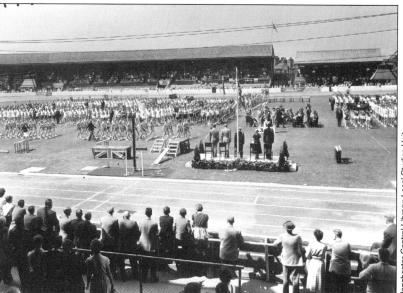

Manchester Central Library: Local Studies Unit

athletics became linked with schools and universities; lovers of trivia might like to know that the racing costume of Sandhurst was silk stockings, white jackets and knickerbockers. Records of achievement were kept even then. At the University Sports of 1876 at Lillie Bridge, M J Brooks achieved an incredible high jump of six feet two and a half inches. £1,100 was taken on the gates that day, a huge sum of money at that time.

Above right: Young men and women proudly march past the judges' podium at Belle Vue Stadium in 1955. Each one was a competitor in the All England School Athletic Championships. Would any of them come near to matching Roger Bannister's achievement made only the year before, when he ran what was later dubbed the Mile of the Century in 3 min 59.4 seconds?

The mid 50s were key years in British athletics. On 2nd June 1955 Glenn Davis broke the 50 second barrier in the 400m hurdles, while Charles Dumas became the first man ever to clear 7ft in the high jump. During the decade that had passed since the end of World War II sportsmen across the board had fought their way back. The declaration of war on 3rd September 1939 had brought an immediate blanket ban on sport, and many sportsmen and women immediately enlisted in the services. It was Winston Churchill's £50,000 campaign urging the nation to cheerfulness that gave sport a new lease of life. Sport meant fun and relaxation, and 'Winnie' himself enjoyed the odd football match. Britain was going to be cheerful; things were once more back on track.

Shopping spree

Running between the Old Market Place and Victoria Street, The Shambles was a popular little street market that dated back many years, and fish and poultry sellers had their little market here at the turn of the 20th Century. Much of the area was flattened during Nazi bombing raids, but street traders quickly re-established their small businesses. The scene in the photograph is typical of the area during the 1960s, and the fruit stall in the picture was possibly situated in the small passage at the side of Marks and Spencer. A good selection of apples, pears, oranges, grapefruit and bananas was on offer at the fruit stall, in fact an advert for Fyffes bananas can just about be made out above the front of the stall. The prices charged by street traders have traditionally been a few coppers cheaper than the larger shops would charge. The lady on the left is obviously a canny shopper, and the purchase she has just made is about to be deposited in her carrier bag. The flowered 'pinny' worn by the trader was popular work wear even in earlier decades when no woman would ever dream of beginning a job without her apron.

Above: 'The Little Hut' was being screened at the Avenue Cinema when this photograph was taken in 1958. Rochdale Road Blackley is rather different today, being the main link between the M66 and Chadderton, and part of the motorway circle runs directly behind the Avenue building. Victoria Avenue goes off to the left towards the large council estate. This terrace of shops and houses in Rochdale Road is still there today. The Avenue was one of the focal points in the life of the tight community, keeping the people of Blackley entertained year after year. Belcher's shop is advertising Players cigarettes and Walls ice cream, and no doubt sold sweets and chocolates as well. The shop would have been a popular stop off before a visit to the cinema. Today, the rustling of sweet papers is hardly heard in cinemas; the tub of popcorn has all but replaced the bag of sweets.

Right: A solitary car waits at the traffic lights at the junction of Market Street, Corporation Street and Cross Street, and the block of shops and offices opposite wears a tired and desolate air. The signs above the shops tell us the reason, and forty years on the wording of the notices still conveys the anger and resentment of the traders in the area that was earmarked for redevelopment. 'Forced out after 50 years' the pawnbroker Prosser & Son's sign tells us bitterly, while Beaty Brothers on the corner spells it out for us: 'Premises to be Demolished'. The desperate protests had no effect however on those who had already decreed otherwise, and within months these old buildings that had served the city well had vanished for ever. Before long the thirty acre site would lose its pubs, shops, banks, hotels and shops and would bristle with tower cranes and scaffolding. A landscaped pedestrian area eventually emerged from the organised chaos to be appreciated by the next generation of shoppers who had never known Market Street as it was in this photograph. Just off picture to the right is the Royal Exchange, which was the centre of Manchester's commercial life for many years.

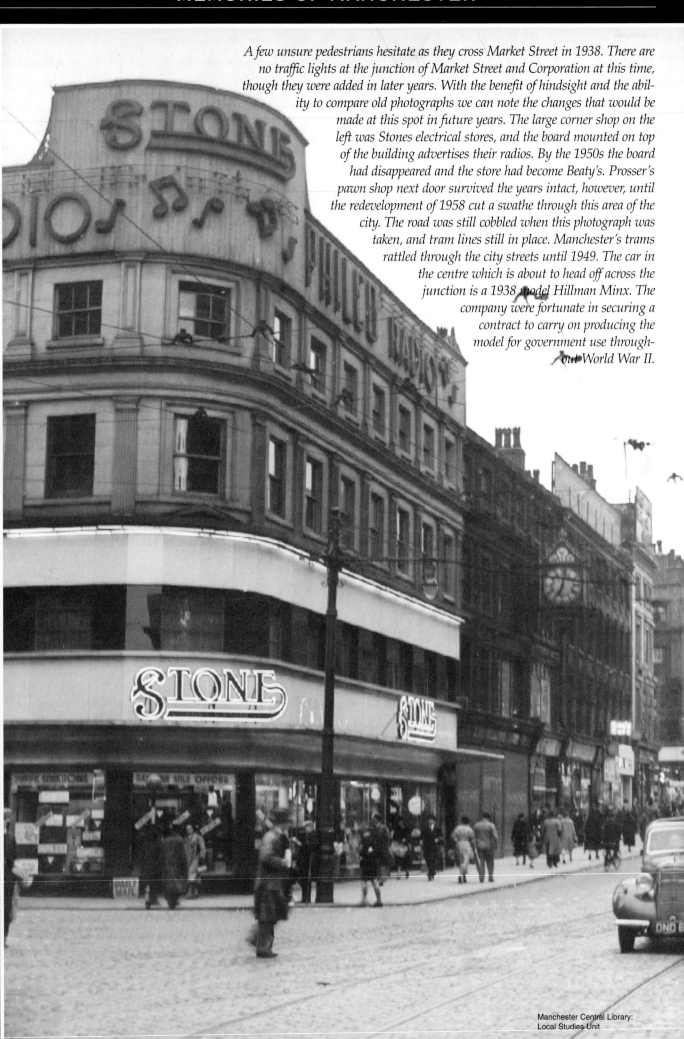

A few unsure pedestrians hesitate as they cross Market Street in 1938. There are no traffic lights at the junction of Market Street and Corporation at this time, though they were added in later years. With the benefit of hindsight and the ability to compare old photographs we can note the changes that would be made at this spot in future years. The large corner shop on the left was Stones electrical stores, and the board mounted on top of the building advertises their radios. By the 1950s the board had disappeared and the store had become Beaty's. Prosser's pawn shop next door survived the years intact, however, until the redevelopment of 1958 cut a swathe through this area of the city. The road was still cobbled when this photograph was taken, and tram lines still in place. Manchester's trams rattled through the city streets until 1949. The car in the centre which is about to head off across the junction is a 1938 model Hillman Minx. The company were fortunate in securing a contract to carry on producing the model for government use throughout World War II.

Above: Many readers will no doubt have fond memories of the Alhambra Cinema in Ashton Old Road, Openshaw. The Alhambra ended up as a typical suburban cinema. Nevertheless the building has an interesting history. Built in 1910 as a theatre, the Alhambra for some time entertained local residents with its popular music hall turns. As the 'talkies' began to gain popularity the management very wisely forestalled the possible defection of their audiences to 'picture houses' by converting the theatre to a dual purpose attraction. The rear of the building became the Pavilion, where films were shown, while the Alhambra continued as a theatre. Alhambra audiences declined, however, and in 1916 the Alhambra became a cinema while the Pavilion was turned into a dance hall! A confusing but understandable move by an obviously enterprising management. In an area of mixed residential, shopping and industrial use that had a number of other cinemas, the entertainment offered by the Alhambra had to meet the demands of the customer. The Alhambra survived until 1960.

Market Street, traditionally one of the busiest spots in the city, has seen many dramatic changes since this photograph was taken in 1957. A No 77 Reddish bus - probably a Stockport Corporation vehicle - waits for the traffic lights to change (note the lack of advertising on the side), while a lovely old car is sandwiched between the newer A30 and the cream Ford. Henry's was the shop on the left with the ornate canopy, and Hope Brothers outfitters had the large corner site. Market Street was always a popular place to shop, made accessible by the nearby Piccadilly Station and the availability of the multitude of trams and buses that passed up and down the street. Manchester's massive redevelopment of the Market Street area in the 1970s added the pedestrianised area, undercover shopping and the Arndale Centre, rendering the street unrecognisable to former Mancunians revisiting the city after a number of years' absence. It was this development, of course, that twenty years later took the force of the massive IRA bomb that devastated the heart of the city on 15 June 1996. 80,000 shoppers and workers were evacuated in time to avoid fatalities, though 200 people were injured.

Five-thirty at the end of another long, hard day, and everybody wants to get home as fast as possible. But no one is going anywhere in a hurry in this traffic jam.... It was 1953 when these crowds of commuters were caught on camera, and in the heyday of public transport chaotic scenes like this were repeated at the end of every working day. Before and during World War II the motor car was viewed as something of a middle class status symbol which was beyond the reach of the ordinary person in the street. In the post war years stability and prosperity was a long time arriving, and for many families in Manchester the private car was still a far distant dream. Fortunately there were plenty of buses and fares were cheap, and whether you were going to work or to a dance you would more than likely hop on a bus or trolley bus. The two Crossley bodied Manchester Corporation buses in the foreground were both on the No 93 Central Station route. During the 1950s fourteen different major operators ran bus services in Greater Manchester, each fleet having its own individual livery. One-man operation was introduced in 1958.

On the move

Manchester Central Library: Local Studies Unit

Manchester Central Library: Local Studies Unit

Above: It was buses like this one that were involved in the evacuation of patients from hospitals that had been damaged in World War II air raid attacks. Equipped with its own stretchers, the vehicles were a useful extension of the ambulance service, and were capable of transporting a greater number of injured people from bomb damaged areas. Parts of the city of Manchester were completely devastated during the war. The enemy made concentrated attacks on the city during the winter of 1940-41, and six hundred people from Manchester and the surrounding area died during the Christmas bombing raids. Whole areas of the city were destroyed; the Exchange Station, warehouses along Parker Street, the Old Shambles and the Old Market Place, Baxendales, Woolworths, the Manchester police headquarters. In June a bomb falling on the nurse's home at Salford Royal Infirmary killed 14 nurses. Mancunians struggled valiantly on during the bombing raids. 'Open as Usual' was a sign often seen while out shopping, while it was not unusual to see 'More Open than Usual' on shattered buildings.

Top: The year was 1959, and car enthusiasts will recognise the familiar Morris Traveller, the Humber, the Morris (Oxford?) and the classic lines of the homely old Ford Popular among the queue of vehicles entering the car park at Old Trafford Cricket Ground. A memorable match had been played at the ground three years earlier in 1956, when Jim Laker, playing for England, got 19 wickets in the Test Match against Australia in July. In the first innings he took ten for fifty-three and in the second he took nine for thirty-seven. His partner Tony Lock took the other wicket. Interestingly, the highest individual score at an Old Trafford Test Match was made by Australian R B Simpson, who scored 311 against England in 1964. In the same match Ken Barrington scored 256 against Australia; Australia made 656 for eight declared.

This photograph, taken in 1946, reminds us of just how popular Belle Vue once was. The leisure complex was often described as the 'showground of the world'; certainly its exhibition halls were at one time the largest outside London. Many of its facilities were closed down during World War II, and parts of the grounds were requisitioned by the government for military use. Much of it did remain open, however, and the pleasure grounds became a mecca for war weary people in search of diversion. Belle Vue was at the height of its popularity during the post war boom between the mid 1940s and early 1950s, when literally millions converged upon the pleasure grounds. Losses that had been suffered during the war were made up; new animals were acquired for the zoo, the buildings were renovated, and more facilities introduced. There had been a pleasure park on the site since 1836, when entrepreneur John Jennison leased the land for six months to develop his ideas for a pleasure garden that would serve the people of Manchester. It took off in a big way, and Jennison established a deer paddock, gardens, boating lakes, a maze, and archery and cricket facilities.

Left: Piccadilly in 1957 was vastly different from the central square with its smart shops and the Plaza Suite that we are familiar with today. But if we go back even further to the pre-war years, Piccadilly was different again, and older Mancunians will remember the warehouses of Staines Inlaid Linoleum, Peel, Watson & Co and J Templeton & Co that bordered Parker Street and Portland Street until the Luftwaffe reduced them to a heap of smoking rubble on the evening of Christmas Eve 1940. That raid was a particularly bad one. Searchlights raked the sky seeking the elusive German planes. The flares they dropped lit up the city as wave after wave of German bombers passed overhead, dropping their deadly load of high explosive bombs across Manchester. The Parker Street warehouses were hit badly, and fed by fractured gas mains the whole row was soon a blazing inferno. Exhausted ARP wardens and firemen worked bravely on though incendiary bombs were falling around them. The blaze raged on for many hours, and eventually it was realised that the only way to fight the fires effactually was to blow up the untouched buildings that lay in the path of the fire.

Below: This was 1957, and changes were being made at Piccadilly bus station. Plans for even greater changes were already afoot that would change the appearance of Piccadilly for ever, placing the Plaza Suite (once described as 'the worst in community development in the 1960s') firmly on Parker Street where a line of warehouses stood before they were destroyed by the Luftwaffe on Christmas Eve, 1940. Meanwhile, life went on as normal, and during the changes hundreds of commuters carried on using the bus station that had supplied the community with public transport for much of the century. Public transport had by the 1950s developed into a reasonably comfortable way to travel, which was not the case in the early years of buses and trams. The design of early motor buses was based on the original horsedrawn omnibus, and their solid rubber tyres, coupled with the cobbled roads of the city, would have given passengers a somewhat teeth chattering ride.

Manchester Central Library: Local Studies Unit

Above: The Ford Motor Company's connection with Manchester goes back a long way. It was 1911 when Henry Ford brought his economical Model T, which he had begun to produce in 1908, on to the British market, and Manchester was the starting place of his operation. The Model T was the world's first really affordable car, and it very quickly became popular. It was Henry Ford who devised the now familiar conveyor belt assembly line in 1913, introducing an eight hour day and offering his workforce a five dollar minimum wage. Ford's factory and shop were in Trafford Park; 100 cars could be produced daily, a steady supply to meet the growing demand for the new mode of transport that was replacing horse driven vehicles. The Manchester Garage in Oxford Road was the city's Ford dealer in 1970. The garage carries no detectable petrol logo, but the driver filling up at one of the half dozen petrol pumps in the photograph would have paid between 6/4d and 6/6d (just over thirty pence) for a gallon of petrol. Ten shillings (fifty pence) would have bought him four and a half pints of oil.

Right: Somewhere along the line Manchester acquired a rather unfair reputation as being the city where it always rains. On this photograph, however, which dates back to 1934, it is the city of fog rather than rain. You might be forgiven for taking it for granted that the picture was taken one dismal winter's evening, but this line of traffic halted by the police officer on point duty (who appears to be taking his life in his hands) was caught on camera in the middle of the day. Thousands of coal fires around the city added their smoke to the fog, creating what came to be known as smog - a deadly mixture of smoke and fog that turned day to night, caused countless traffic accidents, and brought on asthma attacks and bronchial problems. Fog descended on Manchester with monotonous regularity, as it did in all large cities, and the acrid smell and taste of soot hung in the air. Pedestrians resorted to tying scarves across their noses and mouths while vehicles crept along the city's roads at a snail's pace, following the tail lights of the car in front. In 1952 Manchester was one of the first cities to introduce smokeless zones.

A magnificent past and a most promising future

In Manchester there must be few people who have not had relatives or friends working at some time for Avro, the aircraft manufacturers. In succeeding generations they would have worked for the same company after it had been absorbed into Hawker Siddeley Aviation or, in 1977 when nationalisation took it into British Aerospace. Whatever the title, this large family of employees were proud to work for a company which ranks high in the world of aeroplane builders.

The company itself was formed in Manchester on New Year's Day 1910 by Alliott Verdon Roe and his brother Humphrey. It was A V Roe who claimed the distinction of being the first Englishman to fly in a powered aeroplane of his own design just two years earlier. The company trade name of AVRO soon became recognised as one of the leaders in the fledgling aviation industry.

Above: The air-minded 'Daily Mail' sponsored an Avro 504 seaplane to tour coastal resorts during 1914 and after completion the aircraft's engine was test run in the yard at Clifton Street.
Below: The Type E being transported to London Road (now Piccadilly) Station for the train journey down to Brooklands in Surrey for test flying. Brooklands, of course, was the Mecca of the flying pioneers at the time.

Avro's first facility was in the basement of Brownsfield Mill on Ancoats Lane, Manchester and in the early years of expansion moves were made to Clifton Street, Miles Platting and, during the First World War, into one section of Mather & Platts Engineering Company before a move to the custom-built factory on Briscoe Lane, Newton Heath. The great expansion had materialised through the adoption of the Avro 504 as the standard training aircraft for the Royal Flying Corps and, later, the Royal Air force.

In the years that followed, quiet periods saw Avro making billiard tables. prams and even cars, before aeroplanes began to roll off the production line with famous types like Avian, Tutor, Cadet and Commodore carrying the company name around the world.

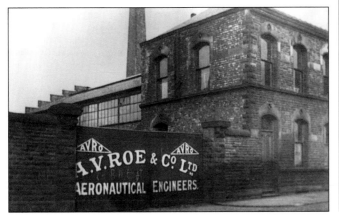

Above: An Avro E aeroplane under construction at the company's first manufacturing facility at Brownsfield Mill in 1912. After completion the aircraft had to be dismantled for transportation to the flying field. The basement at Brownsfield Mill looks much the same today.

Left: Avro was registered as a Limited Company in January 1913 after the large Manchester brewer of Groves & Whitnall Limited invested in the aeroplane company. New premises were soon found in Clifton Street, Miles Platting, with the move from Brownsfield Mill being completed in March 1913.

Below: In July 1912 Avro flew one of its Type 500s to Old Trafford, Manchester to allow the company's employees to see one of their aeroplanes in flight for the first time. The aircraft is shown in a field outside the works of Robert Carlyle Ltd.

Below: *Avro's custom built aircraft factory at Newton Heath was opened just in time to see the end of the First World War and during the next decade business was slow but as new aircraft began to appear, orders rolled in. There seems to be little available space in this shot taken in 1932 with Tutors, Avians and Avro 10s all in build.*

Above: *The great demand for Avro 504 training aircraft during the First World War saw the need for production expansion with Avro leasing a full bay of Mather & Platt's Park Works. Here, 504s await collection from outside the famous engineering works.*

Above: After the famous raid in the Ruhr dams in May 1943, the leader, Guy Gibson and his crew visited the Chadderton and Woodford factories to see Lancasters in production and to meet the people who built them. This photograph shows Gibson chatting with the aircraft's designer, Roy Chadwick. Top: As the Second World War started, Avro was producing a twin-engined bomber named Manchester. However, the unreliable engines forced the company to look at a four-engined version which was named Lancaster and the rest is history! Here, Lancasters await their test flights at Wood ford in October 1942. Right: Avro's had many famous visitors on morale boosting tours but one of the most popular was Mrs Eleanor Roosevelt, wife of the United States President, seen here sharing a joke with Laura Bailey in Chadderton's Tool Room. Also in the picture is Roy (later Sir Roy) Dobson, MD of the company.

In the late 1930s, as the war clouds gathered, another large factory, this time at Chadderton, was opened. The company's airfield at Woodford was also the subject of a massive expansion programme and it was these two sites which contributed most to Avro's war effort. During the Second World War these factories turned out the mighty Lancaster, the 'faithful' Anson, the Manchester and even Bristol Blenheims built under licence.

The Lancaster was undoubtedly the greatest bomber to come out of the war and the Anson was known to everyone who served in the Royal Air Force.

The post-war years saw the development of such aircraft as the Shackleton long-range maritime reconnaissance aircraft which served in the Front Line for over forty years until the last aircraft was finally retired in 1991.

Above: With hardly any space to spare, Chadderton's floor area is completely covered by Lancasters under construction during June 1944.
Right: The post-war years saw the instruction of the mighty Avro Vulcan which provided Britain's nuclear deterrent for over 30 years. This early Vulcan is on test flight over the River Mersey near Liverpool in June 1956.
Below: Vulcans under construction at Woodford in January 1957. The new assembly building has three production lines, each one a quarter of a mile long with the airfield's runways long enough to cope with even the largest of today's aircraft.

and Canada to win large orders from national carriers such as Lufthansa, Sabena, Crossair(Swissair) and a host of others with its quiet and economical operations making it a firm favourite with passengers and operators alike.

Although the company name has changed, the traditions of Avro continue today through British Aerospace as it is still at the forefront of aviation technology. This is its magnificent past. The company - and Manchester - look forward to its most promising future.

One of the last Shackletons forms the magnificent centrepiece of the North West Museum of Science and Industry at Castlefield in the heart of Manchester.

Following the Shackleton came the Avro Vulcan four-jet delta-winged bomber which provided Britain with a nuclear deterrent capability for over thirty years. The Vulcan was a crowd puller wherever it appeared and, as a tribute to this fine aircraft, the company has preserved one at Woodford.

Because of changes in military policy in the 1950s, Avro decided to look at the civil airliner market and produced the ubiquitous Avro 748 to replace the old Dakota. The company sold 400 of this type to 50 countries around the world. Because of its reputation for safety and reliability the 748 was used by sixteen Heads of State as their personal aircraft. First flown in 1960, the Avro 748s can still be seen in many parts of the world providing excellent service for a variety of airline, freight or military operators.

In recent years both woodford and Chadderton have continued in their original roles although in slightly changed styles. Chadderton is an aerostructures facility and, with its excellent reputation, completes work for such famous companies as Boeing and Airbus, Woodford, however, with its massive assembly sheds and excellent airfield, builds the world-beating Avro RJ Regional Jet airliner. This aircraft beat off heavy competition from the United States, France

Above: The Chadderton factory in May 1957 proudly bears the company title. Although built just before the war, the factory never advertised the name for obvious reasons, although the Luftwaffe knew of its existence and proved it by paying a visit on Easter Monday 1941.

Below: The proud traditions of Avro are still evident today and none more so than Woodford's excellent RJ Regional Jet which is in service in many parts of the world, providing passengers and operators with quiet, economical travel. With an excellent order book and continuing interest from airlines, the RJ looks set to break many production records.

The doyen of the motor trade in Lancashire

William Grimshaw was born and bred in Prestwich, attending Park Lane schools as a boy and graduating from cycle making to automobiles in the early days of petrol-driven engines. Long before the First World War he was in business in Radcliffe as a gramophone dealer and introduced that instrument into the public parks for entertainment. In 1909, in Heaton Park, he gave what was claimed as the biggest gramophone concert in the world, with around 50,000 people being present. The music on the records was played by Paderewski and the great man attended the occasion to listen to his own playing and draw the crowds.

Turning his entrepreneurial talents to the motor trade led to the local paper referring to him in 1937 as the 'doyen of the motor trade in Lancashire.'

As a youth he worked and studied hard and he never lost his fondness for the sciences or for

music. It was not until 1882 that he launched out modestly in business for himself and about 1895 he entered the cycle trade. As many cycle traders did in those days, he made bicycles called 'Pinwheels' on his own premises.

Meanwhile he was becoming intrigued with the possibilities of the internal combustion engine and was seduced by them into the motor trade. First he took on the Maxwell car agency in Deansgate. A few years later, this name was dropped by the makers and replaced with Chrysler. His family were all engaged in the firm he founded.

Right: The current showroom in 1926, displaying a selection of new Chrysler cars. Above: Where it all started. Facing Page Top: This picture from left to right is Bill Grimshaw, Brenda Grimshaw, Mr & Mrs Muggleton (Chrysler Motor Ltd) and Percy Grimshaw. Facing Page Bottom: Life before bicycles and motor cars was felt hat manufacturing for the Grimshaw's.

They were proud, in October 1929, to attend the formal opening and housewarming of the new depot in Manchester, Chrysler House at 5, 7 and 9, Cateaton Street. The new showrooms comprised a block of three shops knocked into one spacious hall. Concealed lighting simulated sunlight and 20 new Chryslers were sent to decorate the showroom - and to be sold after- wards, of course.

Soon, "Pa" Grimshaw had made the name a household word on his own and the car's merits.

He handled a huge number of orders.
It is reported that he once sent a telegram to the Chrysler headquarters in London which read, 'Please forward quarter gross Chrysler cars assorted.' The cheque to cover this order was for £11,000. Mr Grimshaw's comment was, 'There was a time when ordering a quarter gross of nipples for bicycle wheels would have given me as much anxiety.'

"Pa" Grimshaw held a record of having been chairman of practically every trade organisation in the old cycling days and he was one of the pioneers of the Motor and Cycle Trades Benevolent Fund. He was also connected with the Motor Shows held in Manchester at the time. He was elected, by national ballot, on to the trade association's Management Committee in London and was very proud of this honour.

He died in his 82nd year of a heart attack and he was much missed by the local people. They had known him as the man who always looked forward, who was never seen without his light bowler and his cigar, who was full of life and good humour and who loved the high-powered car which he would drive at top speed with all due care.

The innovation that kept Grimshaws on the map in 1937 was the 'Turret Top', the trade name for the first sun roof. The management team must have prayed for a good summer that year! This was followed by another first. Grimshaws began selling the first cars with fluid flywheels. These were devices for transmitting power through the medium of the change in momentum of oil. Two opposing fans were fully enclosed in the liquid container. It was similar in principle to a Froude brake in which the stator is released to form the driven member.

War came in 1939. Three years into it, in 1942, Grimshaws signed a contract with the RAF to renovate and repair Chevrolet General Purpose trucks. This kept the workforce more than busy for the duration of hostilities. Grimshaws were among the bidders when the Government held auctions to get rid of surplus Dodge trucks.

In 1956 Chevrolet set up two main dealerships, one in the south and one in the north of England. Grimshaws were appointed as the northern dealers and proceeded to sell Chevrolet vehicles to celebrities such as George Formby, Mike and Bernie Winters and Bob Monkhouse. These classic cars were what the stars wanted. In 1967, the importation of right hand drive Chevrolets stopped.

In 1947 a new Chrysler model with right hand drive was imported for the company's use. Named the 'Chrysler Windsor', it sold well. In fact, during the years from 1948 to 1950, Grimshaws had their best business ever. Because new cars were so difficult to obtain they were selling for up to twice the list price. It was not unknown for customers to arrive at the showroom and bid against each other for the new vehicles available.

In 1968, managing director Bill Grimshaw opened the North West's very first self-service filling station. Potential customers on the first day were encouraged with offers of 3d off a gallon of petrol as well as quadruple Green Shield Stamps. The idea proved very popular and further enticements were unnecessary.

In 1952, Grimshaws joined Vauxhall as what at the time was known as a 'sub-agent'. In their first year, Grimshaws sold 24 new Vauxhalls, a phenomenal number for the time, though a poor showing by the 1990s rate of 2000 a year.

It was decided in 1972 to run a double franchise, so Peugeot was added to

Right: Cateaton Street showroom, Manchester. Above: Clip from a newspaper ad. Top: Original and to this day current location. Facing Page Top: Another newspaper ad. Facing Page Bottom: The Manchester City showroom before moving to Cateaton showroom.

Vauxhall. Business boomed until the oil crisis hit the British motor industry in 1977. Grimshaws' very practical answer to the problems was to rent half of their premises to Kwiksave whilst they carried on their temporarily reduced business in what was left.

In the early eighties Grimshaws entered the fleet market, seeing this as an opportunity for growth as company cars increasingly became the norm. Soon, fleet cars became Grimshaws' speciali-sation, with sales increasing from 100 fleet cars in the first year to 2,000 cars in the fifth. In 1990 a purpose built fleet centre was constructed at Prestwich on the site of the old body shop to produce new cars for the fleet customer. The next logical step seemed to be for the company to prepare for its own deliveries. Consequently, Grimshaws set up a transporter business, beginning

Right: The start of self service petrol in 1968 (Bill Grimshaw stood behind cashier). Above: Grimshaw's first petrol station.

in a small way with a Land Rover and trailer and proceeding through two-car and three-car carriers to the current 35-ton Scania transporter which cost £100,000. It is equipped with a telephone and a fax machine so that it is a travelling office. It has enabled Grimshaws to take on delivery work for other companies.

In 1996 it was decided to stop selling petrol in order to concentrate on the other aspects of the business. The petrol station became a huge used-car operation, with space to display sixty cars.

The company has always been prepared to invest in order to keep up with the most modern technology. Now it has its own website to communicate with customers all over the world.

The firm finds time to share its expertise and experience. Recently a deputation of Slavanian

"IN 1968, MANAGING DIRECTOR BILL GRIMSHAW OPENED THE NORTH WEST'S VERY FIRST SELF-SERVICE FILLING STATION"

Opel dealers has been entertained and instructed. Opel is the trade name of Vauxhall on the continent and the Vauxhall market is much more mature and developed in Britain.

Recently, Vauxhall has reshaped its operation in the UK. Previously, 500 dealers shared the territory. Under the new regime, less dealers are put in charge of bigger areas, though each is required to open a greater number of retail outlets. After a tough selection process, Grimshaws' position has been ratified as the Manchester Northern Market area franchise.

The company looks to the future with expectations of even greater success.

Below: The new self service petrol station in 1968.

Efficiency and reliability win the day

A Mayne & Son Ltd should maybe claim to be more than 78 years old as the family became involved with transport well before the First World War. Arthur Mayne senior is known to have delivered furniture by horse and cart from his shop in the Bradford area of the city. The Maynes also had a general store.

In time, Arthur junior became apprenticed to his upholsterer father, but, when war broke out in 1914 the boy became a medical orderly at the age of 14. After a bout of pneumonia, he was invalided home. He abandoned the furniture business as the toxins it used would have further damaged his lungs.

Instead the family bought a model T van in 1920 in which Arthur junior made deliveries. Arthur's war service had introduced him to the Associated Equipment Company. After the war the sturdy lorries it had produced were adapted for civilian use. In 1923 Arthur bought one. He used the lorry base with a charabanc body to run weekend excursions to the coast and to Buxton.

For a while his motor coaching work was seasonal whilst haulage work for local industries kept him busy all the year. When the coaching work began to include trips to football matches and race meetings, business improved to the point where the haulage work was given up. In 1925 the first purpose built coach was purchased.

For some time, Arthur continually came into confrontation with the Manchester Corporation over licensing. Nevertheless he persevered, buying his first brand new bus in 1929. In 1930 an arrangement was reached in which he was allowed to pick up any passengers who were travelling beyond the city boundary. As the other private bus companies began to disappear Mayne's Pioneer service expanded. The first Regents were bought and the coaching side of the business expanded.

With a growing fleet of double-deckers, a change of premises was needed. Whilst a search was being made, a section of the roof of the old building had its roof raised to accommodate them. Eventually a move was made to Ashton New Road in Clayton in 1939. Trams ceased to travel along that road. In the next few years the Corporation Transport Department made strenuous efforts to take over Maynes' business.

The outbreak of war in 1939 brought Maynes' summer season to an abrupt halt and the holiday services were terminated. Three coaches were

Below: An early pioneer charabanc, fully loaded ready for an excursion. Note the solid rear tyres in comparison to the pneumatic front tyres, this would have been done to compensate for the weight of the passengers over the rear axle.

commandeered for the war effort. Too old for military service, Arthur Mayne became a Special Constable. Fuel was short and there were few qualified men still available for vehicle maintenance.

With the blackout imposed, buses had to be painted with white stripes but night driving was still dangerous.

After the war years the company did its best to put everything right

and business flourished in a quiet way. The increasing costs of labour, vehicles, spares and fuel were absorbed in the post-war boom until the end of the forties. This tailed off however and passenger numbers tailed off in the fifties owing to the increase in personal transport.

The company's first underfloor-engined coaches arrived in 1954, fitted with pre-selective gear boxes and air pressure brakes.

In 1953 Mayne's had taken over the Droylsden Excursion and Tours license from Shipley's of Ashton-under-Lyne. They began looking to extend the catchment area of its tours programme. Four years later the business of F H Dean of Newton Heath was acquired, followed by further takeovers. Maynes' coach fleet now comprised seventeen vehicles.

A new general manager took over Manchester Corporation's Transport Department in 1965. His first proposal was to replace all the trolley buses. As the only other licensed operator of a stopping bus service on Ashton New Road, Maynes objected. a compromise was reached and things ticked over until the Labour Party, very committed to an integrated transport system, appointed the Rt Hon Mrs Barbara Castle as Minister for Transport. Another, and then further attempts were made to acquire A Mayne & Son Ltd.

The family held together and politely declined

Top: A 1930s line-up showing the early Mayne/Pioneer fleet.
Above: A later line-up of the Mayne fleet pictured in 1937. Left: The first new bus that Maynes took delivery of in 1929, AEC's model 660 known as the Reliance.

each offer. Following the death of his mother in 1957, Arthur's wife Olive had taken on the role of company secretary and the couple's eldest son Andrew had joined the board in 1968. His younger brother Stephen joined him three years later. Stephen Mayne was determined to keep the family from selling to SELNEC and through his manoeuvering, even when Manchester City Transport was acquired by SELNEC PTE, Maynes continued to be protected by the agreement they had made with Manchester Corporation.

When, under government reorganisation, GMT was born in 1974, Maynes still quietly went about its business, now nearly fifty years old and on their

third generation of AEC Regent buses.

The late seventies and eighties brought rear-engined buses. The Roe-bodied Fleetlines that Maynes acquired cost £25,000 each. Unlike GMT, the company used multi-coloured destination blinds throughout the eighties, changing to yellow letters on a black background for the 213 and white on blue for the 209 route.

As operating costs continued to escalate the company reluctantly gave up its strong belief in the crew operated bus and experimented with a one-man-operated low fares scheme.

The Transport Act of 1980 began the process of deregulation with the abolition of the need for

licenses on long-distance coach services. Deregulation finally dawned in October 1986. Maynes had 'tested the water' during the semi-deregulated period and fared better for it.

Most passengers who travel the Mayne way will have given little thought to what goes on behind the scenes to ensure their bus turns up when they expect it. To the casual observer, Maynes' garage is just a big shed in which the company keeps its buses. However, a properly run garage, staffed with expertly trained personnel is essential to the

company's efficient and reliable operation. A staff of around 120 is currently employed by the company, including 93 drivers, nine engineers, five cleaners and 12 administrative and operational staff. There are currently 90 vehicles in the fleet, 60 at Manchester and 30 at Mayne's Warrington depot. There is talk of extending the city's Metrolink system and Maynes may once again find itself competing with the tram for traffic along Ashton New Road. History therefore looks set to repeat itself.

Since 1989 the coach division has had its own garage in Fairclough Street, Clayton. The coaches are parked in a large yard adjacent to Manchester's Velodrome Cycling Stadium and the Commonwealth Games site. Modern offices house the coach operations and also deal with the payroll for A Mayne & Son and their associate company Barry Cooper Coaches.

Long-established holiday express services are provided as well as extensive excursions and tours programmes. Private hire forms an increasingly large part of the business, together with regular contracts, for example prison transfers, education authority work, conferences and coach trips to places of interest for foreign students.

The 25-strong fleet therefore is kept very active. When business is overwhelming, Mayne will turn to its associate company for extra capacity.

Recently, one of the company's Bovas was chartered to take a party of local dignatories and HRH the Prince of Wales on a tour of the region. The driving on this occasion was entrusted to the Royal Protection Squad. This was purely for reasons of security and not in any way a reflection on Mayne's drivers' capabilities!

One cannot help wondering what Arthur Mayne would have made of it all now.

Above: One of Maynes fleet of coaches on tour.
Facing page top: Maynes first double-decker bus in Dale Street, while the guard and passengers pose in the rain for the photographer. Facing page bottom: This Duple-bodied Bedford SBG was part of the Maynes fleet from 1958 until 1963.
Below: Recent additions to the Mayne fleet.

The company with the will to win

It was a mere 18 years after Karl Benz first manufactured a 'horseless carriage' that really worked that brothers Harry and Jim Quick went into partnership in the fledgling motor car industry.

Harry had already served a 5-year apprenticeship with the Sale Motor Company, where he was given a thorough grounding in the trade. On his 21st birthday his father gave him a 15hp Fiat Landaulette, and the enterprising young man used the vehicle to begin a taxi service which operated from the Fountain in Ashton-on-Mersey. The taxi business prospered, and it very soon became obvious that the work was too much for one man to handle alone.

It was their father, Tom, who came up with a solution to the problem; he suggested that the brothers should form a partnership. With Tom's help, and for the princely sum of £500, Harry and Jim built a garage at Old Trafford (a building which, incidentally, still stands at the time of writing). The original capital accounts are revealing; Harry's credit was little more than the value of his Fiat while

Jim's account was credited with the grand sum of £4. 9s 3d. The taxis ran a total of 26,300 miles - and the end of year accounts showed a modest success.

The brothers' hard work was rewarded and by the start of World War One in August 1914 Harry and Jim were on the up-and-up; in addition to their steadily growing repair business they were operating a very large fleet of private hire cars, buying and selling cars, and renting out garage space.

March 1914 saw the beginning of Quicks' long association with the Ford Motor Company. It was fortunate for them that Henry Ford had chosen a site in Trafford Park, just a few minutes' walk from H & J's garage, to set up his first UK factory. Ford's Model T, the original 'Tin Lizzie', had already established itself as a firm favourite, and the brothers became agents to sell the Model T. The war dragged on, lasting far longer than anyone had originally expected, but the business was now extended to include provision of insurance and, to aid the war effort, manufacture of munitions in part of the works. A

Above: One of the original taxis in 1916, filled with members of the Quick family. Left: The new service facilities at the premises built on the site of Gresham House.

huge effort was put into war work during 1917, and at the end of the year the business showed record profits.

Interestingly, in January of the same year, a plot of land in Chester Road was purchased; it was this site that was destined to become H & J Quick's headquarters.

The end of the war in 1918 saw a changeover from military to civilian work, and for the very first time the company recorded a loss. Added to this was the fact that the agreement signed on the Chester Road site demanded that they begin development of the site within six months. The brothers rode the tide, and in 1919 they were appointed main Ford dealers, with the right to sell cars both retail and to the trade. The same year saw the ending of the brothers' partnership and the formation of the private limited company, H & J Quick Ltd. With their appointment as main dealers, Harry and Jim faced the major

decision to concentrate their interest entirely in the Ford dealership. It was a good decision; by 1919 Britain had 110,000 cars on the road, and it was obvious that the motor trade was here to stay. In January 1921 the Quicks sold their taxi business - and their one hearse.

Ernie Antrobus, Quicks' much valued Sales Manager, began to look closely at the firm's sales

*Top: H & J Quicks at Old Trafford in 1927, note the solitary petrol pump on the forecourt. **Above left:** Harry and Jim's acceptance of the Ford Dealer's agreement. **Below:** A beautifully illustrated advertisement for the £100 Ford Saloon introduced in 1935.*

It can be yours -

THE £100 FORD SALOON *Ford*

OUR MR. GITTINS
would be delighted to meet you and explain the scope of the Ford Sales and Service that Quicks can offer you in Bury - right on your doorstep.

You will be surprised how much you save in time and money by letting Quicks attend to all your Ford requirements.

Call and see Mr. Gittins at

QUICKS
H. & J. QUICK LTD.

MAIN FORD AGENTS FOR BURY, HEYWOOD, AND RADCLIFFE.

WATER STREET, BURY
Telephone 1347/2

policy. He argued that, rather than have salesmen waste their valuable time calling on all prospects whether promising or not, the company should employ women who would canvass from house to house. Salesmen would therefore only need to call on the good prospects and hopefully conclude the sale. The method proved a success.

The company had its setbacks as well as its triumphs, however. During the 1920s more than 50 vehicles were destroyed in an extensive fire.

Worse was to come. In April 1926 Ford announced that they had outgrown the Manchester plant and production was to be moved to a new factory in Dagenham, Essex. And, moreover, they were developing a new car that would succeed the Model T. Quicks' sales fell dramatically, then ceased altogether. Their response was to collect together all the spare Model T parts that they could find; from these they made around 150 cars. The new Model A had its setbacks and teething problems, and as a sideline H & J opened what proved to be a highly successful motor cycle accessory shop on Chester Road. Around the same time they sold their interest in the Sale Motor Company and bought premises in Bury as a site for a new depot. Very slowly, deliveries of the new cars began to pick up. Those were the days of deep depression, but even so by 1930 car sales were back up to 347.

In September 1931 the last Ford car left the Trafford Park conveyors for delivery to Quicks, ending an era in their history. Quicks might have been the last - but they were also the first: the first vehicle produced at the Dagenham plant on 1st October 1931, a 30 cwt Model AA truck, was delivered to H & J Quick Ltd.

For several years the Quick brothers had been concentrating on opening a number of depots which would take their service to the customer, and by the mid 1930s they had depots in Peter Street, Bury,

Altrincham and Cheadle, and after a number of trials they had also settled on a city centre site at the corner of Deansgate and Peter Street. 'Quick's Corner' became a familiar calling place for the Manchester motorist.

And then war once more loomed on the horizon. Between 1939 - 1945 trade, naturally enough, decreased. As in earlier years, Quicks made its contribution to the war effort, and RAF vehicles were reconditioned by H & J staff. New cars were as rare as hens' teeth after the war, but there was still a profit to be made in general servicing, and a concentrated effort was made to get older cars, that had been laid up for the duration of the war, roadworthy once again.

By the early 1950s the firm was not only back on its feet but was once more flourishing, and in 1953 H & J Quick's turnover for the first time topped the magic £1 million mark.

The following years saw further important expansion: branches were opened in Timperley,

Top left: A newspaper advertisement introducing Norman Gittins, manager of the new Quicks site at Bury in 1928. Below: Quickco - Quicks parts business winning the top performance award for the district in 1987.

Bretton, Ashton, Ellesmere Port, Vicars Cross, Newry Park and Bury. The pattern was set for the future, and in 1986 the firm's profit target (before tax) of £1,000,000 was exceeded by almost 25%.

The family run business was beginning to change by the mid eighties with plans for major expansion which would set the foundations for the group's current status as a nationwide distributor of vehicles and parts.

Customer loyalty is something prized by Quicks, that is why Quicks have always tried so hard to please their customers. With a large market supplying fleet operators they were among the first in 1991 to gain BS5750 quality assurance standard and to extend that to private customers in the used car market.

In 1992 the group celebrated its eightieth anniversary with a tea party for drivers born before March 1912 - being joined by 200 guests with eighty-year old Sir Matt Busby as guest of honour.

In public and business life, Quicks continues to be well represented ranging from the late Norman Quick, high sheriff of Greater Manchester in 1991, and Jim Quick a visiting lecturer at Manchester Business School and familiar local radio voice on business topics, to current chief executive Alec Murray. As chairman of the NFDA, (National Franchised Dealers Association), Alec Murray helped steer the motor trade into the next century through negotiations with both UK and European governments. It produced a strategic viewpoint of

enormous value to Quicks Group and one which will enable them to be in the best possible shape for their centenary in 2012.

Industry awards too have celebrated Quicks' achievement in fields of training, environmental concerns and a multitude for business performance.

When in 1987 Quicks sold its Cheadle site they made a move to the Midlands which established the group's first non-Ford dealership with Peugeot in West Bromwich. This was rapidly followed by Audi-Volkswagen at Oldbury, three Rover franchises in Coventry and Leamington Spa and Vauxhall in Birmingham. In 1993 they bought the Laidlaw group in Scotland and culminating in November 1997 with the £45m acquisition of the southern-based Caverdale Group.

Quicks Group plc, quoted on the Stock exchange since 1947, had now (1999) become one of the country's ten largest motor groups with a turnover of some £600m and over 2,500 employees across some 50 businesses representing 17 marques from Dundee to Bexley.

Original entrepreneurs Harry and Jimmy Quick would be very impressed.

Top: Nearly 200 veteran motorists - all over the age of 80 - helped Quicks to celebrate their 80th anniversary with a tea party at the Old Trafford showrooms in May 1992. Two of Manchester's most famous names were guest of honour, Sir Matt Busby and an original Model T Ford, built at Ford's original factory on Trafford Park.

Williams Motor Company - always delivering a high quality of service

Williams Wheelwright Works was founded by John Henry Williams and began trading in Manchester in 1909, repairing horse-drawn vehicles for London and North Western Railways from his premises in Cornbrook.

Mr Williams was blessed with four sons and six daughters. The eldest, Fred, took an interest in the business and for some time held the job of stores manager. He combined this, however, with selling paint for Beards and, unfortunately, died early, in 1948. Harry was with the CIS for most of his working life, having left the company at an early age. He returned to the fold upon retirement from the CIS at the age of 65, to take up a directorship which he held until 1966. The third son, Horace spent all his working life in the engineering side of the business, bringing the technical

knowledge he had received serving with the Royal Engineers during the war to bear in the company workshops and service departments. Vincent, the youngest son became company secretary, then

and Mr Williams and his sons decided to transfer to motor maintenance. The company started a round-the-clock service, including the use of a converted breakdown vehicle, believed to be the very first to operate in the Manchester area. They soon obtained appointments as official repairers to the leading insurance companies and it was not long before they found the increasing number of customers more than justified their venture.

managing director and finally chairman. He died in 1982 in his 75th year without retiring from the firm. Harry's son Jack served with the company after being demobilised from the army in 1946 until his retirement in 1986.

In 1922 the business had moved to Trafford Street where it was installed in a series of arches under the railway, a seemingly unpromising premises. Despite the handicaps of varying ground levels and curved brickwork, the arches were converted into a compact and efficient self-contained workshop.

By 1926 horse drawn traffic was in decline

The company carried on trading in this small way until 1940 when they started to function as an army auxiliary workshop in conjunction with REME, who were stationed on the site. This type of work continued until after the war, when in 1947 the MOD offered the firm a central workshop in Fazakerley, Liverpool and all government work was subsequently transferred from Manchester to Liverpool. The operation at Trafford Street reverted to private, commercial and insurance repair work

Above: *The premises on Deansgate shortly after completion in 1960.*
Right: *A view of the interior of Williams' newly built showroom on Deansgate in 1960.*
Facing page top: *A heap of rubble covers the site on Deansgate prior to its transformation into 'modern' premises.*
Facing page bottom: *War-time breakdown vehicle and recognisance cars at Whitworth Street West, Manchester.*

service and parts operation and continued to retail used vehicles from its Deansgate showroom. Some five years later they built an additional showroom adjacent to their main site solely for retailing used BMW vehicles. The closure of the Deansgate showroom enabled the company to offer its full range of services on one site.

Today the company represents BMW in both the Manchester and Liverpool city centres. Its operation is hugely successful and has been built on long-established family values. Both dealerships are fully supported by their own independent bodyshop facilities.

and gradually the volume of business increased due to the return of post war private motoring.

In 1960 the company opened their car showroom in Deansgate for the purpose of retailing new and used cars under the Rootes franchise, and in 1970 the current BMW franchise was acquired. By this time the bodyshop side of the business had moved from Trafford Street to new premises in Hadfield Street, from which it continues to operate today.

BMW continue to be at the forefront of vehicle technology and Williams are committed to supporting the franchise by delivering a consistently high quality of service to all of its customers.

They realise that, to remain successful they need to continually change to meet the ever increasing demands of their customers.

Above: An exterior view of the prestigious premises on Upper Brook Street. *Below:* The interior of the 'high tech' new car showroom.

Another branch of the company, known as PSV was opened in 1973 to convert vans to mini-buses and coaches. Production was operated from Liverpool but the sales division was in Manchester. The initial success of this branch was due in no small measure to the introduction of the breathalyser test by Barbara Castle. Fear of prosecution gripped the public and pubs, clubs and hotels were all arranging their own transport.

At first, Williams had this branch of business to themselves. Later, through competition in this sector of the market, Williams' share dropped and the company decided to consolidate production and sales back in Manchester. PSV continued to trade until 1996.

In 1984, the company built a prestigious purpose built facility on Upper Brook Street. They transferred the new car sales,

At work

Above: The Auxiliary Fire Service did a lot of sterling work alongside the regular Fire Department during World War II, and the green engines of the AFS could often be observed at the scene of an air raid. High explosive bombing would destroy property, fracturing gas mains and creating huge fire storms that were fed by the often flammable contents of warehouses and shops. This 1939 photograph shows an inspection of the AFS and their appliances. When a fire was reported, often by one of the fire watchers who were recruited from those men who were either too old to fight or were in a reserved occupation, the petrol operated pumps seen here would be towed to the scene of the blaze and would pump water from a nearby dam or a supply of static water. During the war the basements of bombed out buildings were often deliberately flooded to provide a static water supply for the use of fire fighters.

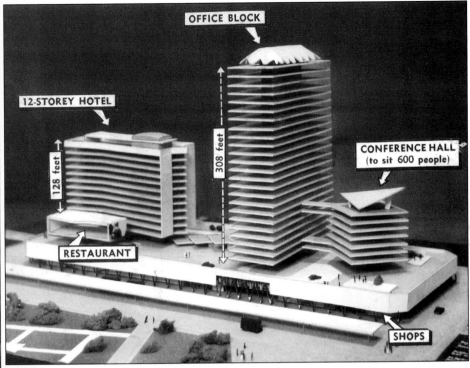

OFFICE BLOCK

12-STOREY HOTEL

128 feet

308 feet

CONFERENCE HALL
(to sit 600 people)

RESTAURANT

SHOPS

Manchester Central Library: Local Studies Unit

Above: The Piccadilly Plaza as it once was - a model made to scale from a set of plans on the architect's drawing board. And the real thing doesn't look all that different from the planners' grandiose scheme for the rebuilding of Piccadilly.

The site was, of course, that of the row of warehouses along Parker Street destroyed by German bombs on 23 December 1940. Fire fighters had battled for fourteen hours at a time to put out the blaze; the fire was eventually controlled by the use of explosives but their efforts to save the buildings had been hopeless from the start. Little remained at the horrific scene of destruction except the gaunt and blackened skeletons of buildings, gaping holes in the ground and heaps of still smoking rubble.

After demolition, the site alongside the bus station was used as a car park for many years until the plans for the Plaza Suite became a reality.

Left: Traditionally, British men have been regarded as the bread winners, going out to work every day to keep their wives and families. Their women folk saw to the children, shopped for food every day, made the meals, cleaned the house, and washed and ironed the family's clothes. The Second World War changed the way of life for hundreds of men and women, turning generations of tradition upside down. When Britain's men were called into military service, women found themselves doing jobs they had never done before. Many of them worked in machine shops and engineering factories, turning out armaments and aeroplane parts, work that had always been looked on as 'jobs for the men'. Women did a good job - and what is more, they found themselves enjoying the work. After the war many of them didn't want to give up their jobs and go back to their old lives. They had become used to the degree of independence that a weekly wage gave them. Suddenly they could afford to buy clothes and makeup and treats for the children.

These women captured by the camera worked in a Manchester ordnance factory, and are seen here turning the shell caps.

Above: The cars have moved out and the cranes have moved in, and the notice by the gate of what was by this time a construction site reminds drivers that as from the 19th April 1960 the Piccadilly car park would be closed. Many readers will remember the city's famous square the way it looked back in 1960; the workmen's sheds that sprouted like mushrooms, the piles of equipment, the huge tower cranes lifting heavy blocks into position, the noise, the bustle - and here and there a few bars of the latest popular song whistled by a passing builder. And was it all worth it? The resulting Plaza Suite was controversial from the very start of its life; some loved it, a lot more hated it, but at least nobody ignored it. Nearly forty years on the Hotel Piccadilly with the Plaza Cafe below, the Sunley Tower office block and Bernard House are showing their age and looking decidedly the worse for wear. Why is it that the modern 1960s 'angular block' developments seem to age faster than the timeless old Victorian buildings?

Pedestrians pick their way gingerly around road works in Piccadilly in 1957 as more changes were made to the square. In the last hundred years or so Piccadilly has seen more changes than most places, yet incredibly is still recognisable in spite of its fringe of modern angular buildings. Younger Mancunians can scarcely visualise the square without its gardens, and many of them would be surprised to learn that the Manchester Royal Infirmary once stood on the site. The Infirmary, which included a 'lunatic asylum', was built in 1755 and dominated Piccadilly, the clock on its dome a well known landmark. The building has all but passed from living memory today, but the Infirmary served the citizens of Manchester well until it was demolished in 1908. Even during the process of demolition an accident and emergency room was kept open in Parker Street. King Edward VII opened the new Royal Infirmary out on the Oxford Road in 1909.

A very fine jam she got them into!

In 1872, Fred Duerr, aged 24, married Mary Eva Naylor, aged 16. In her small kitchen in Heywood, Mary made jams and marmalades for her husband, family and friends to enjoy. Their reputation for quality was well known within the locality. Fred, originally a leather-dresser by trade, was moving up the career ladder and had just started to work as a grocery commission agent.

In 1881, Fred met with a buyer from the Heywood Co-operative Society who was experiencing difficulty in obtaining jams of high quality. There were no laws at that time about honest and complete food labelling and all kinds of unsavoury 'fillers' were being put into the jam he was being offered. The buyer had heard of Mary's jams and asked if Fred would consider supplying the Co-op. (These days, one hopes, he would have asked Mary!) From that chance meeting the family business was born.

At first Mary did all the cooking in the family kitchen and Fred delivered the jams to the Heywood Co-op in a handcart. Business flourished as demand grew, until manufacturing premises were required.

Fred raised the capital to build and equip a small factory at Deanhead, Guide Bridge, Manchester which is still standing in the nineties. A publication of 1890, 'Century's Progress', described it. "Every part is filled up in thorough style with plant and apparatus of the latest and most improved description."

Here Fred joined his young wife in the full time production of preserves. He was a member of the Corn Exchange which he attended every Tuesday. He attributed his success to careful fruit buying and the application of scientific principles to jam making.

In 1890 Duerr's manufacturing

return but time was found to take them on works outings to Blackpool to enjoy the funfair and donkey rides. The women in the factory wore long starched aprons. When times were hard in their personal lives, Duerr's were supportive and this too was not taken for granted. The workers knew when they were well off and most of them served the company for many years. Perhaps Mrs Emily Deakin holds the record, going to work for Duerr's at the age of 14 and finally retiring at 74.

Innovation and quality have always been the cornerstone of Duerr's philosophy. They pioneered vacuum sealing in 1905 while many competitors were still using cardboard caps and paper tissues until the 1950s! The company managed to survive two world wars and the depression and continued to grow from strength to strength.

levels outgrew their Guide Bridge premises and Fred commissioned a purpose-built factory on Prestage Street, Old Trafford, the site the factory still occupies today. He employed Mr A Pearson to do the work which cost him £1,315 16s 4d. This did not include the cost of manufacturing equipment which he had made to the highest standards. In 1903 Duerr's spent the sizeable sum of £148 on a new Cornish boiler, installed by J K & R Lord of Bury. Then, in 1906, Fred had a telephone system installed in time for the busy summer fruit season.

The company was well known and well appreciated for the generous wages they paid to their staff. Hard work was expected in

Top left: Staff take to donkeys on a staff trip to Blackpool in 1905. Top right: Workers waiting for the visit of King Edward VII to Trafford Park. Above: A 1914 advert for Duerr's high class preserves. Right: A group of women employees in their long starched aprons pictured in 1910.
Facing page top left: Mary Duerr who provided the recipes and the inspiration for the family business. Facing page top right: Fred Duerr who founded the business along with his wife, Mary. Facing page bottom: A recent picture of Duerr's first factory.

Fred's youngest son Edgar was something of an inventor and came into his own during the First World War. During the Boer War, Duerr's had sent out tins of jam to the Lancashire Fusiliers, but in 1914 the company completely changed direction and put its expertise into manufacturing to support the war effort. Edgar invented and patented a collapsible pocket periscope for use by soldiers in the deadly trench warfare. The periscopes were extremely sturdy and were responsible for saving many lives.

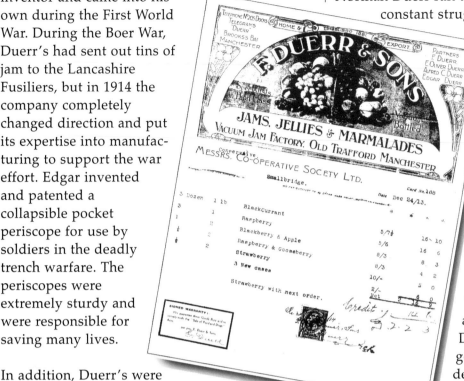

In addition, Duerr's were the first company to use tamper-evident 'button caps' and shrink sleeving on their range of products.

During the Second World War, Edgar's nephew Norman Duerr ran the factory. It was a period of constant struggle to obtain the strictly rationed sugar and other raw materials. Before the days of easy freezing, all fruit, of course, had to be processed immediately which made planning difficult. There were also labour shortages as skilled workers were conscripted. Spare parts and machinery were in short supply even when the war was long over.

The early sixties were another very difficult time as Duerr's wholesale customers got together in groups, depriving the company of much wholesale distribution. Things got so bad that some shareholders recommended closing down the business. However, Duerr's secured the contract

to pack VG Preserves and later, in the seventies, Kwik Save put Duerr's on to their shelves and helped to make it the national brand it is today. Now, 90% of Duerr's UK trade is with the multiples and exports go as far afield as Greece, Gambia and China.

In 1989 the company diversified from their mainstream jam and marmalade production by entering the peanut butter market. A new, purpose-built peanut butter production line was built at prestage street, and Duerr's started to supply the major multiples with crunchy and smooth

varieties under their own label, the Duerr brand and the Whole Earth brand of peanut butter.

To cope with the ever-increasing demands for storage and production, in 1996 the company invested in a new warehouse and second production site in Wythenshawe. The 70,000

Above: Jam production the old labour intensive way.
Left: *The print of fruit from the 1920s still in evidence today as part of Duerr's corporate identity.*
Facing page top: *A typical early invoice from 1913.* **Facing page bottom:** *A selection of vacuum sealed jars, pioneered by Fred Duerr in 1905.*

Duerr's market share has steadily increased over the years as the company's reputation for quality jams, marmalades and peanut butter has grown. Today, Duerr's products can be found all over the world as the company exports to almost thirty countries.

The company throughout its existence has been generous to many

square feet site houses all the raw materials, together with the finished product. In 1997 Duerr's completed the installation of a specialist production line in order to satisfy demand for a new range of jams in which more whole fruit pieces were retained in the finished product.

charities. Perhaps the most unusual event happened in 1989 when Mr Tony Duerr, with the aid of an aircraft and seven friends, raised ten thousand pounds for charity by playing four full rounds of golf in Scotland, Ireland, Wales and England in one day, beginning at four in the morning and finishing at ten o'clock at night.

It is likely that the speed of change in the industry will accelerate, but the company, with its heavy investment in the latest technology and skilled personnel is looking forward to meeting the challenges of the next century. In readiness, all employees have taken, and passed, a course in Food Hygiene. Duerr's has recently been awarded BS 5750, an internationally recognised certificate of excellence for quality management in business.

Duerr's remains very much a family business and a member of the Duerr family has led the company since its inception. This has ensured that the traditions so lovingly begun by Mary are adhered to today, with the emphasis on high quality ingredients, innovation and manufacturing excellence.

Above left: Mr Tony Duerr proudly displays his O.B.E. for services to the food industry presented to him by Her Majesty the Queen in 1995. Above right: 'Seriously Fruity' a new range of jam launched in 1998. Left: In a bid to win a new generation of fans, Duerr's introduce Paddington's Special Orange Marmalade in July 1998. Facing page top: Ladies at work in the glass feeding department. Facing page bottom: Part of today's Jam production area.

Tantalising tastes from all over the world

Duckworth & Co (Essences) was founded in 1885 by William Duckworth when he was only 24 as he started to demonstrate his remarkable aptitude for developing and marketing high quality flavourings and novel ways of producing them.

The business was originally established at 93 Corporation St, and prospered over the first 10 years to the extent that by 1895/6, he was able to design and build the familiar Distillery on Chester Road, Old Trafford. The company, now more commonly known as The Duckworth Group,

continues to use this imposing Grade II listed Victorian building as its international headquarters which was fortunately saved from destruction by incendiaries during World War II by the efforts of the company fire picket in preventing flames spreading from the roof because of the 9 inches of sand that had been carefully spread throughout the top floor for just this eventuality!

Originally Duckworths specialised in flavours for the soft drinks industry and an early price list included lemonades, limes, gingers, cream sodas, sarsaparilla, bassera, hot tom, nutmeg, vanillas, peppermint, quince, caraway and of of course colas! In 1928 the company had a well publicised legal tussle with The Coca Cola Corporation of Atlanta, over the generic use of the word cola for which well known trade marks were being claimed!

The company has always had a strong export trade and records exist of successful visits to Japan and Hong Kong as early as 1909, with other business being developed in India, South America, the Caribbean and S E Asia in the 1920s. By the time the company celebrated its centenary in 1985, 40% of its turnover was being exported and since then it has successfully developed three joint venture manufacturing facilities in Shenzhen in China, Bangalore in India and Cape Town in South Africa.

This overseas expansion was supported by a product development programme which widened the focus to include specialised flavours for frozen

confectionery, sugar confectionery, bakery, alcoholic beverages and savoury foods and so today the company's "Heart Brand" flavours are to be found in many national and international food and drink products.

Duckworths is now the largest privately owned flavour business in the UK, employing 150 people primarily in the North West. The Manchester Distillery was recently modernised and is now mostly devoted to marketing, research, product development, flavour application and sensory evaluation with laboratories containing state of the art analytical equipment with teams of highly qualified flavourists and food technicians.

All production has been transferred from Manchester to a purpose built factory on the banks of the Ship

Canal at Runcorn, and where more recently, the production site has been doubled in size. There is also a small, specialized unit at Erith, near London.

The Duckworth Group's success for over 100 years can be attributed to supplying its customers with unique products - mostly specially developed to meet a specific requirement, attention to detail and high quality technical and delivery services. Customers are treated as partners and Duckworths work closely with them to develop innovative products to meet ever changing consumer tastes. The company has over 2500 flavour formulae on its computers and regularly uses 1500 raw materials - many of them natural - from which to draw on.

The company's mission is to be the natural first choice of its customers, by providing consistent and cost-effective products, innovative applications and value-adding ideas. The Duckworth Group has been ISO9002 accredited since 1991, received the Investors in People Award in 1997 and is currently working towards World Class status. The Duckworth Group was one of the first flavour companies to have a web site which can be viewed at www.duckworth.co.uk.

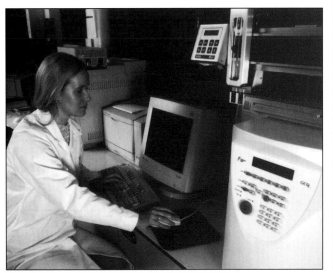

Left: Gas Chromatography Mass Spectrometry equipment.
Top: Part of the original process for extracting flavourings from essential oils.
Above: Modern distillation equipment.
Facing page top: An early view of the Distillery circa 1910. Facing page bottom: A selection of laboratory mixing and filtering vessels at the turn of the century.

Providing an excellent service

James Allcock began his business, J Allcock & Sons Ltd, in 1924. The company started in Audenshaw then in 1928 there was a move to Soapery Street, (later to become Textile Street), in West Gorton.

These premises were on the site of a former wood yard and a Chapel. Mr Allcock turned the Sunday School building into a warehouse for his business which provided chemicals to the emerging rubber industry in the Manchester area. The business was incorporated in May 1928.

The Second World War was a profitable time for Allcocks. The availability of natural rubber was much reduced, so demand for factice (a rubber substitute) was high and profitable. The high demand for proofed fabric meant that Allcocks could sell all that they could make.

The founder's two sons continued the business, but the third generation had other interests. One of the founder's grandchildren, for instance, is James Allcock the Radio Vet who also writes magazine articles about animals. The family business was sold to the Anchor Chemical Company in Clayton. Before starting his own business James Allcock had worked for Anchor making factice.

Anchor ran its new purchase as one of its subsidiaries and used its facilities to make various factices. These rubber substitutes are used in the manufacture of soft rubber compounds such as erasers, proofed fabrics and hoses.

As well as the production of factice, Allcocks started to sell other products required in the rubber industry. This process was continued and extended by Anchor who used Allcocks as a trading house for distributed products that would appear to present a conflict of interests with distribution agreements they had.

Mr R S Rushton, who eventually became chairman, worked his way up in the company from a post in the laboratory at Anchor Chemical, through the position of works director. He became responsible for the running of Allcocks and decided to buy out

Top: J Allcock Snr., extreme left, and J Allcock Jnr., third left. Above: J Allcock Jnr., front with his motorbike. Left: James Allcock Junior who founded the business along with his father James Allcock Senior.

the company and run it with his wife Margaret. At the time the Rushton family took over, the firm consisted of a very small 3-office building, the original warehouse, a second warehouse, a works and a porta-cabin used as a Canteen. Mr Rushton ran the concern with three other staff and one part-timer.

Five years later, Allcocks acquired Truscott (or Diamond) Transport Company and its property next door. The building consisted of a large warehouse with a pit for servicing lorries and a set of offices. The Rushtons installed the Print Room, the Sample Stores, the Workshop, and a Boiler Room. A loading bay was cleared to build a Laboratory. Since the pit in the warehouse floor used to fill with water from the Corn Brook each night, it was filled in. Later, the loading area, over which Allcocks had right of way, was also purchased.

Above: The factice manufacturing team in 1973, from left, Jim Holmes, Joe Cuttle and Ted McCarley. **Left:** *One of Allcocks wagons with a pallet of reclaimed rubber imported from Czechoslovakia.* **Below:** *Ronald Rushton signing a distribution agreement with the worlds largest silicone company, Dow-Corning in 1973.*

Allcocks had its eye on an area of waste land to the rear of their site and bordered by Ambrose Street. Originally it had held a Starch Works, then the Openshaw Brewery had its facilities there. Later still a corrugated paper factory had a four-storey building on the area. After long and protracted negotiations Mr Rushton finally took out the lease option on the site in 1980, which in March 1990 was converted into a 99 year lease. In 1984 a building on Ambrose Street was purchased. This had been the Vaughan Pulley Company. Here they set up a rubber grinding and granulating facility to recycle cured scrap rubber.

Subsequently new offices were added and three production lines installed. Then an electricity substation was incorporated that gave the company up to half a million watts of power.

Unfortunately the Ambrose Street Works was destroyed by fire in May 1992 as the result of arson. Those responsible were never found. The fire started on the roof over the workshop. The pitch on the roof melted through and dropped

into the storage area on to 110 mt of rubber crumb (dust) and granules. The resultant fire devastated the building. The insurers even wrote off the foundations. As well as the building and its contents, it demolished three fork lift trucks and a travelling overhead crane. Though damaged by smoke and water, the offices survived.

It took 3½ years to settle the insurance claim before plans for the future could be made. The Works were rebuilt, on the Ambrose Street site, the two buildings being put up by Williams Tarr. Meanwhile business had continued in rented premises in Mossley and thus a minimum customer base was retained.

At the same time sterling fell out of the ERM and, as the majority of distributed products were

Top left: Land acquired in 1980 for the expansion of the company.
Top right: The fire which destroyed part of the factory on the 16th May 1992.
Left: The new crumb plant.

eries of the correct material on the right day, with the right paperwork and at an economical price. By working closely as a team, the staff benefit by keeping customers

imported, prices went up by 20% overnight. The company survived all this and emerged stronger and more focused.

Today, the company is still deeply involved with the rubber industry but it also distributes compounding chemicals into plastics and surface coatings. It acts as the UK distributor for a number of companies. The firm imports products from the Czech Republic, Italy, France, Belgium, the USA, Sweden, India and Malaysia. It also grinds and granulates rubber scraps so they can be recycled, using what they consider one of the most modern grinding facilities in the UK.

As far as possible, Allcock is a 'green' company. It is in the process of installing another recycling line. Then, it hopes to be able to take the ground material and improve its quality by reversing the curing process, by using a revolutionary product called De-Link R®. This allows the customer to utilise a much higher percentage of recycled material without adversely affecting the quality of their final product.

In a competitive market, J Allcock & Sons Ltd offers its customers an excellent service on all levels. They provide problem-free deliv-

and customers benefit through the service they are offered and through knowing they are valued. Mr and Mrs Rushton retired from the day-to-day running of the company in 1989 although Mr Rushton remained as the company's chairman. Mr Bob Howard ran the company until his retirement at the end of 1996.

Now the company is run by two of Mr Rushtons sons. Andrew Rushton is the Managing Director and David Rushton is the Works Director. They are keeping the tradition of good service going and have attained ISO BS EN 9002 registration and are currently working towards Investors in People.

Top left: Mr Rushton, the Chairman of the company pictured with his wife Margaret. Above: Mr Andrew Rushton, the current Managing Director. *Below:* An aerial view of the premises as they are today.

A Colourful Business

Ciba

Dyestuffs have been manufactured in the heart of Manchester for well over 100 years. When The Clayton Aniline Company was founded in 1876 - Alexander Graham Bell had just invented the telephone, General Custer had fought and died at the Battle of the Little Big Horn and Queen Victoria had just been declared Empress of India.

It was a time of invention and change as Britain became the engine-room of a rapidly industrialising world. New manufacturing processes, new industries and new forms of factory-based employment drew people towards the growing cities of the north of England.

As Manchester emerged as the heartland of a rapidly expanding cotton industry, a 21 year-old chemist, Charles Dreyfus, travelled from Alsace to work for a Manchester firm of textile printers. Just seven years later, with a group of friends, he decided to set up his own business manufacturing aniline textile dyes.

He found the ideal location - a one acre site in a largely rural area of east Manchester alongside the Ashton Canal. The canal ensured a plentiful supply of water, the key raw material in dye manufacture, as well as providing a readily available method of transporting the company's products - through the 92-mile network of canals surrounding the city and then to the Leeds-Liverpool canal - together forming the motorway network of the late 1900's.

Within a few years, The Clayton Aniline Company was exporting its dyes as far afield as Central Europe, Russia and the United States - establishing a pattern of international trade which has continued right up to the present day. Over 90% of all the textile dyes manufactured at Clayton today are exported throughout the world.

In 1911, a new chapter in The Clayton Aniline Company's history began with its association with Ciba - and the Clayton site became the Swiss company's first manufacturing base in the UK.

Above: Charles Dreyfus set up The Clayton Aniline Company Limited in 1876, which manufactured aniline oil and aniline salt.
Below: Dr Dreyfus (seated centre) and members of staff in 1890.

Despite many changes over the intervening years, this association with Ciba has continued - though recently taking a slightly different form.

Ciba Specialty Chemicals became a newly independent business as the result of the merger of Ciba and Sandoz to form a new life sciences business - Novartis. In early 1997 Ciba Specialty Chemicals, Ciba's world-wide industrial chemicals interests, was demerged from Novartis.

The new company is made up of six divisions and manufactures a wide range of chemicals world-wide - from lubricants and inks to materials which enhance the look and feel of textiles and paper; from polymers used in paints and coatings to colour pigments used in the automotive, printing and plastics industries.

Two of these businesses operate from the Clayton site:

● **Consumer Care**
Consumer Care's products include whiteners, antimicrobials, specialty colours and fabric finishes which are tailored for the producers of consumer goods. These materials enhance the performances of products ranging from detergents and cosmetics to paper and textiles. In the UK, Consumer Care's manufacturing operations are based at the Clayton site where they employ over 120 people.

● **Textile Dyes**
Textile Dyes' products are used by the fashion, home and industrial textile industries to colour natural and man-made fibres. Clayton's output is sufficient to dye around 350,000 tonnes of cloth - enough fabric to make a two-piece suit for every man, woman and child in the United Kingdom, Italy, Spain and France. Also, six out of every ten cars manufactured have interior fabrics which use dyes manufactured in the heart of Manchester.

The sales force and customer service laboratories are based at Macclesfield but the majority of the division's 450 UK employees are based at Clayton. Investments of £25 million in recent years have ensured that modern technology and chemical processing maintain the world-wide competitiveness of its products.

Top: A billhead from the early 1900's.
Right: The development of dye production started in this building where Nigrosine, the black dye used for boot polish, was made.

The octane enhancer necessary to achieve this higher octane rating gave them a vital power and speed advantage over Messerschmitt 109s during the long summer days of 1940 and helped brave young flyers win the crucial battle for supremacy in the skies over Britain.

Clayton and the Community

When The Clayton Aniline Company was first formed, east Manchester was a largely rural area. Over the years, the company's site has grown to 57 acres and is one of largest single manufacturing sites in the city of Manchester. At the same time a densely populated residential area has grown up around the site.

The company's long association with east Manchester is matched by an equally close and long-standing relationship with the local community. The company and its employees have always helped, supported, and been actively involved in local schools and community organisations.

Around the world, Ciba Specialty Chemicals manufactures in 29 countries, has more than 23,000 employees and sales of 7.8 billion Swiss francs (1997).

Called to the Colours

The Clayton site has been called upon to serve its country twice during the course this century.

Between 1914-19, as the First World War raged in the fields of France and Belgium the site manufactured the explosive TNT to help the war effort.

In the Second World War, the site produced centralite - a stabiliser for explosives - on behalf of the Admiralty. It also manufactured monomethyl-aniline, a valuable anti-knock additive for aviation fuel, which enhanced its octane rating and played an important role at a crucial stage of the conflict.

The 990-horsepower Rolls-Royce Merlin engines of Spitfires and Hurricanes, for example, were unique in being specifically designed to run on 100 octane fuel.

Its Community Matters newspaper, reporting on local events, is published regularly and distributed free to 8,000 households around the Clayton site. The company also hosts community meetings on a regular basis.

Over the years, there have been many examples of the commitment of both the company and its employees to the local community. One recent example was a donation of several thousand pounds to the East Manchester Community Boat Project to complete the building of a purpose-built boat to provide leisure trips along the canal network for local schools and community groups. The cash value of the donation had been earmarked by the company as a celebration of its achieving the Investors in People Award and, rather than use the cash to buy individual gifts, employees voted to support the boat project. A few months later the canal boat was officially launched by the Projects patron, Bill Roache, Coronation Street's Ken Barlow.

Clayton and the Environment
The Clayton site has always maintained the highest standards of environmental management and has chosen to measure its progress against recognised standards.

The site helped to pilot BS7750 in the UK (which later became the international standard for environmental management systems, IS014001) and Clayton was one of the first chemical sites to become registered under the European-wide Eco-Management and Audit Scheme.

This means Clayton's performance is subject to the discipline of external scrutiny in addition to its own internal monitoring and reporting procedures. The Clayton site has a long-term commitment to environmental communications, having published an annual Environmental Data Report since 1991.

Above: The new gas fired boilerhouse.
Below: Entrance to the Clayton site as it is today.
Facing page top: A view of the works around 1918.
Facing page below: An aeriel view of Clayton site as it is today.

A Solution for every Problem

Great Grandma Markus was quite a character. The business that her husband John started up was not exactly the kind of thing the average young lady would have wanted to get involved with at the turn of the century. Other women might have been content to play the piano in the drawing room or to take afternoon tea with a neighbour. But John Markus' wife was a woman of a different calibre. She had a thread of steel running through her, and she was one hundred percent behind her man. If that meant getting her hands dirty then so be it.

The year was 1902, and John Markus had found a niche for his particular talents. He found that tyre scrapings dissolved in solvent made an excellent rubber adhesive, and when painted onto the outside carcass of the tyre formed an ideal priming coat on which the tyre tread could be bonded. Working from an attic in premises in Cheetham Hill, he set up the India Rubber & Tyre Company. It was his wife, however, who had the job of walking down Deansgate to Knott Mill to collect the tyres for processing. Over her shoulder the tyres would go, and the valiant young woman would trudge back to the house bowed down with her heavy burden. After the tyres had been treated she would carry them all the way back again.

One of John Markus' original formulation notebooks survives, and a page from the old notebook reads like a book of magic spells: a few ounces of antimony, a pound or two of sulphur, a gallon or so of naphtha; add whitening, zinc oxide, magnesia, litharge and a touch of bag black for colour, and there you have it - only without the eye of newt and toe of frog.

Despite the march of polymer science, a number of the ingredients used by the company for today's rubber solutions have remained the same through the years, though naturally the equipment and the technology has kept pace with the times.

Eventually the India Rubber & Tyre Company began to outgrow the attic, and John Markus opened his first factory in Clowes Street in Salford. The firm was on the up and up. Large mixing vats formed the largest percentage of the firm's original equipment, and as India Rubber and Tyre Co Ltd expanded the equipment and the materials became more complex.

Eventually changes in tyre manufacturing techniques meant that the company had to find a new outlet for its products. At that time in the city of Manchester there was a thriving industry developing in the manufacture of raincoats. The process of making waterproof fabric from rubber proofed textile had been invented by Charles Macintosh some 90 years earlier and the siting of his factory in Manchester had spawned over 50 manufacturers of rubber proofed coats. In order to be fully waterproof the seams of the coats had to be treated with a 'varnish' which was 'schmeared' onto the seam by finger and a tape made from the same material placed on top. This was an area the India Rubber & Tyre Company were at home in, so they seized the opportunity. They were not alone in the field. Each firm had its own technique for putting the rubber into solvent, and there were subtle differences between the end product of one manufacturer and the next. There were about half a dozen of such companies who met each year to fix prices in the Manchester area.

This was a family firm in the true sense of the word, and its women were determined to play a key role. In time John's daughter Mrs Irene Ross joined the firm, as did her daughter Anne after her.

When war broke out in 1939, it was Irene Ross who continued in her father's footsteps. During the war the general shortage of materials became a real headache to the firm. One of the company's customers gave Itac the timely help that they needed, however, by managing to secure the contract for the company to provide the army with ground sheets. The ongoing order proved to be a real break, and the contract continued to the

end of the war and beyond.

Right: The first formulations book, covered in a black leather case with a small pencil holder.
Below: Jack Headley, Cliff Skinner with brother Syd celebrating the delivery of a new van -1948.
Facing Page: Company founder, John Markus in the rubber stock room -1912.

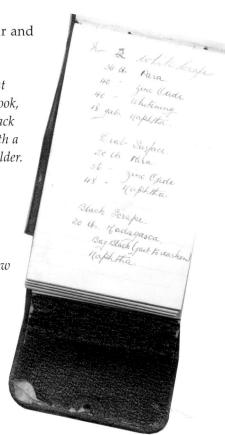

It was after Mr Alan Armitt joined the company in 1954 that it experienced a further stage in its development. He introduced polyurethane technology to the firm. Polyurethane came into the factory in the form of granules. It was put into solution which was sold to the textile coating industry. The solution was not for the seams alone, but this time to give the textile itself a waterproof coating.

The company made a second move to premises in Blackburn Street in Salford, and it was there that the India Rubber & Tyre Company made a more defined move towards expansion.

The acquisition of an adhesive manufacturing business in 1970 led to a change of name to India Rubber & Tyre Adhesives Co Ltd, which was shortened to 'Itac', today's logo, in 1972 when the company moved to their present site in Farnworth, just outside Bolton.

Alan Armitt introduced a marketing strategy which realised the full potential of Itac's mixing equipment, and began to manufacture adhesives in addition to coating solutions.

One dreadful March day in 1988 fire swept through the plant, completely destroying much of its equipment and materials. Bloodied but unbowed, Itac turned the disaster around, and when repairs and renovations got underway the company took the opportunity to re-equip the plant with the latest mixing technology.

Links with the textile industry have survived through the years, and almost half the company's sales today are involved in supplying technical textile coatings. The coating solution when applied to the fabric, dries to a tack free film and can render the textile waterproof, fire retardant or resistant to chemicals. Alternatively the film can be pressure sensitive in nature as used to make surgical dressing.

From the humble beginning in an attic room in Cheetham Hill Itac have become an internationally known company with superior manufacturing techniques. Itac products are used in Europe, the Middle East and Scandinavia, and exports form around twenty percent of their turnover. The company are sensitive to the needs of today's markets, and their customers are largely textile related. Other markets include the building adhesives sector who in turn distribute through DIY outlets and Builders Merchants, together with applications in general industry.

Today's rapid pace of change in the manufacturing industry demands a dedication to research into new methods, machinery and materials. Committed to providing the bespoke manufacturing service that many of their clients need, Itac's team of technical staff have developed the ability to interpret customers' requirements correctly, and can offer them an individually developed product that complements their own method of manufacture.

Itac is proud of its products but it is equally proud of its committed technical and sales support, the high quality of its service and its competitive prices.

The early 1990s proved to be a difficult time for Itac. There were internal problems to deal with in addition to the necessity of facing the general recession. In September 1991 a stroke brought Alan Armitt's involvement with the company to an untimely end, and his son Paul Armitt took over the reins of the company a few months later, in January 1992. His father's day to day input, however, was sadly missed.

Determined to go forward, Mr Paul Armitt placed a great emphasis on bringing the company up to date, and during the 1990s a brand new computer system was installed, the factory and offices were refurbished, and the company image was given a complete face lift. Since then they have concentrated on building up a team of skilled staff with the determination and expertise to drive the company forward. Mr Paul Armitt has now been with the company for twenty three years.

In January 1998 Itac acquired the European quality standard BS EN ISO 9002: 1994 and are working towards an Investors in People assessment in early 1999, all of which will provide them with further opportunities for growth and expansion while continuing to support their existing markets.

And what of the future?

Building on the solid foundation of their many years of experience and the expertise of their workforce, Itac are actively pursuing opportunities for acquisitions as well as organic growth. The overall plan is to grow and develop the company and to go forward into the next millennium providing an extended range of clients with the same high standard of service that has always been provided by the company that is totally dedicated to success.

Below: Mark Tatlock supervising the new production line after the fire - 1988 .
Facing page top: Irene Esther Ross who took over from her father when he died in 1928, having never worked at the factory before.

Matching Industry and the Environment

A family firm in the true tradition, H Marcel Guest was founded in 1930 by two young salesmen, Harold Marcel Guest and Herbert J Falder. After finding suitable premises in Oliver Street, Openshaw, they went into business together to manufacture a bottle capping solution that was used to seal corks in bottles. Once the solution was applied, the result was a plastic cap that moulded itself to the shape of the bottle. Leakproof and tamperproof, the hermetically sealed cap turned out to be invaluable not only to the wines and spirits trade but also to the drugs industry. Available in a wide range of colours, it was also attractive and colour-codable. The fact that the plastic seal was unaffected by extreme temperatures made the product suitable for use all over the world.

HMG spent a short time at the Oliver Street premises before moving to the 'New Era' works in Fitzgeorge Street, Collyhurst, where they were to

discover that the old stable house was haunted by the ghost of a long-dead coachman - a fact which no doubt enlivened the working day of the employees! Harold Marcel Guest left quite amicably shortly after the move to Fitzgeorge Street. Herbert J Falder's father, Benson Falder, left the police force to help his son through very difficult times. The company gradually got onto its feet, moving into the automobile refinish business in an unusual way. HJF's Ford 8 car was damaged by a railway wagon horse, delivering to the company and HJF made his own black cellulose lacquer to repaint the car - the work was carried out by Manchester Garages, who liked the material and promptly ordered five gallons, thus becoming the first customer in that finish.

The success of their first venture into a new field meant that before long the fledgling company was offering an impressive list of other products

including primers, lacquers, synthetic undercoats and stove enamel. The advantages of the cellulose lacquer was that it quickly dried to a fine high gloss finish that was durable and resistant to yellowing and could be burnished and polished.

World War II proved to be a trying time for the company, but unlike many other firms who lost many of their young men and women, all of HMG's workforce returned safely. Raw materials were of course in very short supply during that time and on ration. It was wisely decided that as there were limited amounts of materials available it was prudent to sell them in the smallest possible form, hence the move into model paints. One of the ingredients used in the process in those days was old cine film; a far cry from today's production processes that use thousands of different materials from all over the world.

With the growth and success of the company and the diversification of their products, the type of client they served began to vary widely, from coach builders and vehicle re-painters to pencil makers, with all industrial stops in between, a truly complete industrial paint manufacturer was created.

They naturally offered standard off-the-shelf products, but developing special paints and specialised coatings to complement their clients' products became part and parcel of the company's growing technical superiority.

Now producing a vast range of coatings that are appropriate to any job, and possessing one of the largest turnovers among privately owned industrial paint producers in the UK, HMG today have 200 employees - though they still run the business on the lines of a large extended family. In fact the present managing director John Falder is the grandson of founder Herbert j Falder, and his brother Stephen is Marketing and Export Director. Their father Brian Falder ran the company for over 40 years and is now semi-retired, though he retains the post of Chairman.

This extended family atmosphere has generated the kind of loyalty among their staff that is rarely seen, especially within the larger companies. But HMG regard their workforce as their greatest asset, and greatly value their knowledge and expertise - an

Above: The "haunted" coach house/store. **Facing page top:** *The New Era works, Fitzgeorge St, Collyhurst.* **Facing page bottom:** *The very first big machine purchased new for H. Marcel Guest, a 26" "keenok," state-of-the-art grinding technology in the 50's and 60's.*

attitude that has resulted in an impressive record of long-serving employees. Outstanding amongst this group was Stan Wallwork, who started as a young boy, stayed with the company for 60 years and was honoured by receiving the BEM for his services to industry. This was seen as being received on behalf of all the long serving HMG employees.

A vast range of coatings are produced at the firm's Riverside Works in Collyhurst Road, and in a process that is semi-automatic, the plant and equipment produces quantities of paint that can vary from one litre to 10 tonnes.

The company's extensive customer base lists such impressive names as Rolls Royce, The Rover Group, Ford, The Henley Group, Vickers, GEC, British Aerospace, GKN, Disney and a large number of other major international blue chip companies.

While supplying the large companies, HMG still give total commitment to the individual customer. One of their specialities is colour matching to the exact requirements of their clients, and occasionally they receive rather strange requests for customised materials. They well remember the farmer who

wanted to enter one of his pigs in a show, and approached the company to ask them to produce a pink non-toxic paint to disguise a blemish on its back. HMG matched the paint to the pig - and naturally, the pig went on to win the contest trotters down!

Since the very earliest years of the company, HMG have been committed to innovation, utilising the latest technology in administration and production. Almost 70 years have passed since then, and HMG have developed into independent specialists. The expertise of their large team of knowledgeable staff has allowed the company to offer their clients a technical helpline to their laboratory personnel.

Recently the company's expertise and unique technology went into developing an anti-foul paint from a process that mimics the skin of a living creature. The observation was made that fish and other water-dwelling creatures, in spite of spending 100% of their time in water, are not prone to fouling by marine growth. That simple consideration provided the inspiration for the development of the paint, which they gave the descriptive and highly individual name 'Slippy Bottom'.

woodland, and a total of 1800 native saplings have already been planted. Further phases, to be completed over the next five years, will produce a pond and marsh with timber decking; pathways, hedgerows, meadows, seating and more sculptures are planned. The entire creation will be an area of outstanding beauty which will be available for all to enjoy.

The company have also given sponsorship to a book based on the natural history of the River Irk. A guide to the public as well as an educational tool, the book will be used to further National Curriculum local history studies. Local primary school children will be involved in many of the projects that are expected to result from the book's publication.

HMG are justifiably proud of their commitment to community and environmental concerns, and as a member of the Mersey Basin Campaign have achieved a gold award as a 'good neighbour' for the River Irk. It was the enormous amount of work the firm carried out along the river side, clearing debris and reinstating the riverbank, as well as their meticulous clean water practices, that led to them receiving the coveted award. An ongoing ecological survey by a well-known environmental consultant records the local flora and fauna, and each summer HMG employ a group of students to remove the invading knotweed, an insidious growth that impedes the spread of native flora, from the riverbank.

This culture of care about the environment and towards their employees, suppliers, customers and the local community reflects the traditional values of this family owned firm. HMG thrive on establishing and maintaining good relationships with all who come into contact with them, and their aim is to continue to provide a friendly, speedy and efficient service to every customer anywhere in the world.

Top: The aerosol filling plant handles production runs of up to 10,000 cans. **Above:** *A leaflet for 'Slippy Bottom', Guests new exclusive paint for boat hulls.* **Below:** *The factory as it is today.* **Facing page top:** *Stan Wallwork BEM as a young man.*

The company have an eye to the visual effect of the local surroundings, and they have agreed with the local council to maintain the land opposite their administrative block, employing a member of staff especially to work on the grass and shrubbery. For the benefit of the public as well as their staff, they commissioned several works by local sculptors which they have positioned on the riverbank, on the bridge and within their own grounds, and stone steps with a sculpted handrail leading to the river have been constructed.

Their latest project, to be completed in five phases, will create an area of

Quality and innovation around the clock

It seems difficult to imagine that the nationwide group of companies operating today with sixteen countries for nine thousand clients was the result of the hard work and expertise of one, football-mad man, Paul Hauser.

Paul, a native of Basle in Switzerland, was born in 1895, the youngest of eight children and excelled at school in mathematics, languages and, above all, sport.

He completed his International Transport Apprenticeship with Goth in Basle and, in his spare time played football for FC Basle. He was offered a job with Witag in Zurich, with promotion if he would transfer as a player from FC Basle to FC Zurich. While playing for FC Zurich, they became the Swiss football league champions in 1924/25.

Later he worked for Danzas for eight years, before moving to England. It was whilst he was working in Manchester that he decided to start his own freight company P Hauser & Co.

The Second World War caused him to operate deep sea trade out of Liverpool using convoys protected by the Navy but in 1945 Paul Hauser transferred the operations back to Manchester, starting business in the front room of his semi in Timperley, assisted, part time, by his wife Helen. Then followed subsequent moves to Finnigan Buildings in Brazennose Street; Rhodesia House, Princess Street; Whitworth Street West and finally

to Trafford House in Stretford. Each move being a necessity as the number of staff increased needing larger office space. He began again to develop the Company's services to Switzerland and Central and Eastern Europe. Traffic picked up quickly but the traditional sea routes were slow.

Hauser knew the answer lay with 'direct' rail services, a brand new system that should make it possible to ship from Manchester in as little as ten days door to door. Intending to use this system, Hauser introduced the first export train ferry groupage service to the continent from the North of

Above: Paul Hauser, founder of the company. **Left:** *The Swiss Football League Champions of 1924, FC Zurich, with Paul Hauser pictured seated right.*

England, leaving Trafford Park on December 24th 1946.

The first direct railway wagon took five weeks to arrive at destination. Many marshalling yards throughout Europe were out of commission, some partially, some totally. Using his knowledge of languages, Hauser was able to track down the worst affected yards and choose a route avoiding them. Within three months he was reliably delivering from Manchester to Central Europe in ten days, a fine achievement for the forties.

Communications were difficult. An international telephone call had to be booked with an operator and it could take most of a day to be connected. Tracking a truck or pre-advising a movement was done by telegram. The arrival of telex was a boon but it was still connected by the operator and few clients were on the network. P Hauser & Co was one of the first on telex in Manchester and certainly the first freight forwarder. At first the machine was considered 'spooky' and two of the staff would always walk out of Hauser's office when the telex sprung into life on its own!

> **"USING HIS KNOWLEDGE OF LANGUAGES, HAUSER WAS ABLE TO TRACK DOWN THE WORST AFFECTED YARDS AND CHOOSE A ROUTE AVOIDING THEM"**

Below: A Hauser ISO container being transhipped at Parkeston Quay for the maiden voyage of Seafreight Liner 1 to Zeebrugge driven from Manchester by Michael Hauser in 1968.

Chemical Industries in the North were quick to see the benefits of such services. Soon, P Hauser & Co began to secure lucrative business for the bulk movement of chemicals to and from the European mainland.

The Company acquired its own rail depot at Ardwick East Goods Station in Manchester. In 1952 the Company became P Hauser Ltd and for the next 15 years its train ferry groupage services enjoyed continued success and were expanded to serve destinations in France, Belgium, West Germany, Eastern and Southern Europe and the Middle East.

Paul Hauser was instrumental in persuading UK exporters to sell on freight-paid terms at least up to the frontier of the end user This allowed price comparisons to be made by importers without the need to guess or calculate the possible costs . For the importer, the fluctuations of freight costs were avoided whilst the exporter maintained control of his products right up to the country of desti-

nation. Fifty years on these principles still hold good.

In response to the increase of tankwagon traffic the Company opened offices in London and Harwich to deal only with these movements.

The sixties brought competition from road transport. P Hauser Ltd responded by sending a Hauser trailer to Basle in Switzerland. By the seventies the road trailer operation covered most of Europe. Import traffic increased in ratio with the increase in the network of partners. In 1973 the Company opened an office at Stanstead Airport where the fast airfreight clearance facilities could be used for trailers arriving from the continent.

Paul's son, Michael Hauser has dual nationality. After two years' National Service he spent six years abroad learning his father's trade and becoming fluent in the relevant languages. He became Chairman of the Group in 1981.
In the same year the Company moved to a new

This picture: One of Hauser's Depots working hard through the night. *Above:* Michael Hauser with his mother on his 60th birthday.

depot at Manchester International Freight Terminal and to new offices in Trafford House.

The trailer boom in which Hauser had played a major part had inevitably caused train ferry groupage to decline. In the late seventies and early eighties the Company strengthened its UK network. A clearance office at Dover, and new offices and a depot at Walsall were opened. A Bradford office followed in 1983.

Meanwhile the Southern office had been equally busy with its own import and export trailer services.

In 1985, to encourage regional development, each operational division was given Limited Company status, these being 100% subsidiaries of Hauser Ltd.

Expansion continued, new premises being opened in Sheffield, in South Yorkshire, Romford in Essex and Cannock in Staffordshire in the remaining years of the eighties. More building was done in Bradford in the nineties and in 1995 Hauser Forwarding Ltd came to Trafford Park, bringing all operational and warehousing staff together to concentrate on freight forwarding and logistic contracts.

Paul Hauser proved that expertise rather than capital was needed to start a successful business. He had the business acumen to specialise in specific markets and modes of transport. Today Hauser still concentrates on what it knows best - overland

services to and from Europe from seven strategically placed locations in the UK.

With a £17 million turnover, an expected 100,000 consignments in 1998 and experienced, loyal employees, the Hauser Group serves directly 1,600 customers in 43 locations in 16 countries on a regular basis. The Company's strengths are reliability, speed, frequency and competitiveness.

Hauser staff spend in excess of 70 man days per year travelling throughout Europe and Turkey in the development of new services, increasing of frequencies and learning about local conditions and opportunities.

Under the direction of the founder's son, Michael Hauser, the Hauser Group ranks alongside Britain's leading forwarding agents and operators with an exceptionally strong network of partners.

Top: One of the most modern units at Manchester West Point, Trafford Park. **Below:** *An international delivery to Switzerland.*

Continuously developing to stay at the forefront of the chemical industry

The origins of chemical manufacture at the Manox site in Manchester are linked to the former national coal gas industry, and it is no coincidence that three gas holders on the Eastlands gas works site are visible from the General Manager's office window.

The sale of coal gas was commercialised in the UK around 1800 and the first recorded use of it in Britain was the illumination by gaslight of an engineering factory in Birmingham. Soon afterwards most large towns had a gasworks and a rapidly-growing environmental pollution problem to go with it.

The original Manchester Oxide Company was established in 1864 for the purpose of extracting chemical residues from coal gas extraction. A wide range of derivatives was manufactured from these by-products for sale into the chemical and allied industries. Four years previously the Lancashire Tar Distillers Company had been established and in 1897 Hardman & Holden Ltd was set up to acquire it. Josiah Hardman of Milton, Staffordshire, and John James Holden of Higher Broughton Manchester had formed Hardman & Company to acquire from the Official Liquidator a chemical manufacturing and dealing business, Bouck & Co. The two partners brought different qualities and experience to the business. Mr Hardman was a practical tar distiller. Mr Holden had controlled the Globe Cotton Spinning Company with mills in the Rossendale Valley and in Macclesfield. This well-known company had been highly profitable until the 'cotton collapse' just after the First World War. Mr Holden had been educated at Owen's College which was later to become part of Manchester University. He had spent his business life in the years when Manchester was possibly the greatest manufacturing centre in the world. Like many previously successful cotton manufacturers, he had to look for other investment opportunities and turned to chemical manufacturing.

Mr Holden was capable and successful but he found partnership with Josiah Hardman difficult. They soon formed a second company with George Henry Holden as third partner to operate on a site in Clayton. In 1892, the two partnerships became the limited company, Hardman & Holden Ltd. with Mr Holden as chairman. Josiah Hardman retained a small interest but sold most of his shares to his brother William. William Holden attended board meetings and drew handsome dividends until his death in the 1920s.

Certificate No. 86874.

The Companies Acts, 1862 to 1948.

COMPANY LIMITED BY SHARES.

Memorandum
AND
Articles of Association
OF
HARDMAN & HOLDEN
LIMITED

Incorporated on the 5th day of May, 1892.

BOOTE, EDGAR & CO.,
Manchester, 2.

Above *Messrs Hardman, Holden and Clayton*
Left *Hardman & Holden's Articles of Association.*

In 1892 H&H as the family called the firm, bought the Manchester Oxide Company for £999 precisely in settlement of a bad debt. It proved a fine investment, for which much credit was due to Robert Henry Clayton, a nephew of John Holden, and his son James Holden Clayton.

*Left: Staff and their "transport" pictured outside the works at the turn of the century. **Below:** Hardman & Holden's exhibition stand at the Royal Jubilee Exhibition, Manchester in the late 19th century.*

offices were the business centre with the adjacent tar distillery operating in addition to a second tar distillery on the Clayton site. The tar distillation side of the business was sold in 1926 with the activities becoming part of the Lancashire Tar Distillers Ltd. By-products of the coal gas production included cyanide ammonia and sulphur. These chemicals were extracted and purified at the Miles Platting site. The cyanides were processed to produce a range of ferrocyanides leading to the production of iron blue pigments. The ammonia was distilled for sale and also converted to sulphate of ammonia for agricultural use after neutralising with sulphuric acid. The sulphuric acid being produced on the site by a company called

In the same year, the Manchester Corporation took H&H to court for 'noxious emissions', and attempted to close the business down. The firm was a relatively large employer and so the smell of sulphuretted hydrogen continued.

Until after the First World War the main activity was tar distilling which had become an important industry following the significant growth of the coal gas industry in the early 19th century which was originally developed for gas lamp lighting of streets. The works were strategically located in Varley Street, midway between the two principal gasworks. The works were on either side of the Rochdale Canal, connected to the gas works by underground pipelines which delivered crude tar. This arrangement continued until the 1960s, though all traffic on the canal had stopped by 1930.

Part of the site in Miles Platting was in use as a chemical works as early as 1820 producing dyestuffs. The name of the owner at that time, Nicholas Varley, is commemorated in one of the approach streets to the site. At first the main activity was tar distilling. The strategically placed Varley Street

Right: *An interior of the state-of-the-art Manox plant.*
Above: *A young managers meeting at the Grand Hotel, Manchester in 1937.*

CJ Schofields after burning the sulphur in a 'Lead Chamber' sulphuric acid plant. H&H acquired the Schofields business in 1956 when the old acid plant was closed and subsequently constructed a modern 'Contact Acid Plant' on the Clayton site.

The success of these and other developments is indicated by the fact that, at its peak in 1955, HARDMAN & HOLDEN LIMITED was a major employer in the area with some 900 people actively engaged in chemical manufacturing activities.

In 1947 H&H became a public company through the placing of a proportion of the shares on the London and Manchester Stock Exchanges.

Above: An aerial view of the Manox plant site in Miles Platting.

Following commercialisation of natural gas from the North Sea in the sixties, production of coal gas in the UK ceased. It had provided useful employment, both directly and indirectly, for many thousands of people for over 100 years, including the chemical processing of its by-products.

For the company, 1960 began an association with Borax, a new parent company involved in mining. Borax were interested to diversify into chemical manufacturing operations. In that year, the company ceased production of carbon disulphide and thiourea and the Pendleton site closed. By 1968, Borax had merged with Rio Tinto Zinc Corporation plc. and in 1973 RTZ Chemicals Ltd was formed. This led, in the following year, to the dissolution of H&H and the formation of

Degussa ◈

Manchem Ltd and Manox Ltd. Over the next few years the manufacture of sulphuric acid and sodium hydrosulphite came to an end. The Biddulph colour works belonging to Manox Limited closed ending production of Aniline black and Lake red C pigments with production of iron blue pigment being transferred to the Miles Platting plant.

By 1988 Manox Ltd was fully integrated into Manchem Ltd, the Northern Division of RTZ Chemicals. Then, in the following year, RTZ Chemicals Worldwide Group of Companies was bought by Rhone-Poulenc for £2.4 billion.

In 1990 Degussa AG, a leading chemicals concern with precious metal and pharmaceutical sectors headquartered in Frankfurt, purchased the Manox plant site from Rhone Poulec to cosolidate its own position in the iron blue pigments business.

The Clayton site has continued to be developed by Rhone-Poulenc and is now one of the Group's major manufacturing site's in the U.K. Since 1st January 1998 the site has traded as Rhodia Limited a member of Rhone-Poulenc Speciality Chemicals Group.

Left: An aerial view of the site in Clayton.

The leading independent distributor of chemicals in the UK and Eire

The Tennant Group was founded in Scotland in 1797 by Charles Tennant of St Rollox, who found a safe way of harnessing the bleaching power of chlorine by passing chlorine gas over slaked lime to create bleaching powder.

Until this time, the bleaching of cloth, prior to dyeing, had to be done by spreading the cloth out in the open air to be bleached by the action of the sun and the wind. This process took several months. The use of bleaching powder reduced the time to only a few hours. Soon a thriving business had been built with a number of chemicals being manufactured, mainly for textile processing.

The textile interest led to the establishment of distribution branches for the linen industry in Belfast and Dublin. In 1830 Tennants (Lancashire) Ltd was formed in both Liverpool and Manchester where materials were brought by the Tennants' schooner fleet into Liverpool and taken by rail for the cotton trade. This continued for many years with a thriving company based in Manchester throughout the turn of the Century. In the 1920s Tennants manufacturing units were sold to form The Imperial Chemical Industries Ltd. This was necessary to produce a British chemical company sufficiently powerful to hold its own in a market dominated by Germany and America. Around this time, Sir William Alexander, whose father and grandfather had worked for the Tennants since the earliest days, bought the distribution companies from the Tennant family. The new owners then added to the distribution companies by developing and purchasing many manufacturing companies who now manufacture products such as Formaldehyde, Oxides, Pigments, Resins and Dyestuffs.

As the largest independent distributor of chemicals in the UK the Group acts as agents and distributors for many of the World's chemical manufacturers. Apart from general chemicals, the distribution companies supply specialities from their Textile, Resin, Food Ingredients and Plastics Divisions. The company recognises the need to offer a full service to both customers and suppliers and, as a consequence, offer dilution, blending and packing facilities for third party products. These facilities are used by some of the most well known names in the Chemical Industry.

In addition to its expanding distribution business, Tennants are actively engaged in exporting chemicals and dyestuffs to the EEC countries and the rest of the World. They are also large importers handling the distribution of chemicals, dyestuffs and resins for various overseas manufacturers.

Above: One of Tennants' fleet of distribution tankers.
Below: An aerial view of the Lancashire site.
Facing page top: Sir Charles Tennant, Bart.
Facing page bottom: The St. Rollox Works, Glasgow, 1844.

Their sites are equipped with modern bulk storage facilities, enabling them to supply solvents and chemicals in everything from tankers to mini bulk tanks, as well as in smaller containers. Automatic drumming is available, embodying up to date technology and outstanding health and safety features.

The Group ensures that all its facilities conform of the best possible practices and are under continual review to ensure that they conform or exceed all new standards. The Group are members of the Responsible Care Programme operated within the Chemical Industry. Their expertise enables them to offer advice on handling chemicals safely.

From a traditional plumbers to a complete property refurbishment service

In 1908, plumber John Mills decided to set up on his own in his trade. He took premises in Blake Street, Hulme, Manchester which were part of the original Rolls Royce factory and remained there until 1962 when the building was destroyed by fire.

With John Mills as managing director and Joe Broster as company secretary, the business flourished. Following the Second World War Jack Mills joined the Company.

By 1962 the company had come a long way, but this was the year in which everything went wrong. Following the death of John Mills, his son Jack took over the Company and things seemed to be looking up a little when temporary accommodation was found following the fire. However, Jack Mills was taken ill with tuberculosis and following a long illness the future of the company was in doubt. Jack Mills survived the illness and the company began to recover.

The stay at the temporary premises lasted for four years, after which there was a move to Castle Street, Knotts Mill. The Company had its headquarters here when Peter Mills joined the family business in 1977.

Ten years later, Jack Mills retired and, in the same year, 1987, a further move was made to Cornbrook Street, Old Trafford. In recent years, under the influence of Mr Peter Mills and the current management team of Ian Nolan, Gary Solomon and David Selby, the traditional emphasis of this family concern has changed. Plumbing is no longer the chief activity and service. Now the firm's clients come to Mills for services in property refurbishment and maintenance.

Left: The Company founder, John Mills pictured in 1909 the year after he founded the Company. *Above:* Jack Mills in his RAF uniform, pictured during the war, after which he joined the Company.

Customers include the Royal Mail, Lambert Smith, Hampton, Jones Lang Wootton and DTZ Debenham Thorpe. The Company has recently made another move to Jardine House on Elsinore Road, Old Trafford where they hope to consolidate and expand the business.

Due to the family nature of the business it is common for craftsmen to stay all their working lives, so that their experience builds into craftsmanship. Messrs Bill Clarkson and Harold Redwood both retired in the 1990s after more than thirty years' service with the company.

The Company's chief customers these days are the major breweries and work has been done for Whitbreads, Bass Taverns, Joseph Holt and Inntrepreneur.

A run down public house is handed over to Mills for complete refurbishment. A recent example of this work is the Cross Guns Inn. The Company also specialise in maintenance for a variety of commercial clients.

Above: The Company's first premises on Blake Street, the name J Mills can just be made out to the right of the lamp standard. Below: The Cross Guns pub recently refurbished by J Mills.

Tackling the millennium challenge

Unglamorous and prosaic as it might sound, lifting tackle is nevertheless the key to efficient and safe production and is therefore vital to industry throughout the UK.

The need for good lifting gear was first recognised during the Industrial Revolution, and necessity, as everyone knows, is the mother of invention. In 1830 William Dale, a young chainsmith from the Black Country, addressed the need, setting up a chain repairing works in Vesta Street, Ancoats. From repairing and refurbishing chains, he eventually moved into actual manufacture, and later expanded into nearby premises in the same street.

Little is known today about William Dale himself and the early history of the firm, but the founder established the tradition for good craftsmanship and customer service that Dales has been proud to uphold throughout the company's 170-year-long history.

The last century saw the Whitehead connection made with the firm, when a Mr McGowan joined the company, later passing control of the company to his son-in-law, who in turn left his interest to his brother-in-law, Mr Newman. Mr Newman's daughter Dorothy and her husband Jack Whitehead later joined the business. In 1959 the firm became a limited company, Dale & Company (Ancoats) Ltd.

Dale's handling and lifting products have long been designed to meet the UK's industrial needs, and they have developed a strong emphasis on safety. As the firm made their mark in the industrial world their achievements were many. The company was both a

founder and a continuous member of the Lifting Equipment Engineers Association of Great Britain (formerly the Chain Tester Association of GB), and in 1987 they became the first firm in the north west of England to achieve BS Part 2 in their field. In 1997 they set up a computer link between Manchester and Preston to enable them to produce accurate computer drawings; this led to their achieving in 1998 the prestigious ISO 9001.

In 1990 the continued success of the company led to a branch being opened in Preston, mainly to house the equipment centre and sales office.

One would naturally assume that the giants of the construction industry, civil engineering, and those in

Dale & Co's concern for customer care has given them prestige in the industry, reflected in the long service of some of their key staff members. Works Manager John Wright, for example, has been with Dales for 26 years and Malcolm Owen 36 years.

The company operates a continuous staff training programme that enables them to offer in-depth advice about safe handling and lifting, and in the similar vein of customer care they have established a 24-hour service for their clients in the event of crane or lift breakdown.

So much for the past, with its successes and triumphs. But what will the future bring for Dale & Co?

The company's involvement with Ancoats now spans almost 170 years. Yet plans are afoot in Manchester which, if successful, threaten Dale's links with the area. Manchester, as host to the 2002 Commonwealth Games, is planning to build a huge new Sports Stadium with a tramway link planned to run from the city centre to the proposed site of the stadium. Dale & Co's problem is that those provisional plans route the tramway link right *through the centre of their factory.*

Faced with the compulsory purchase of their premises, the old established company are determined to take up the challenge that faces them and not only survive but thrive in the new millennium.

Above: Jack and Jacqueline Whitehead with Dale's BS 5750 award in 1987. Below: A specially designed crane leaving Dale's Factory. Facing page: Three men around a forge.

plastics and timber would form a large proportion of Dales customers - as they do. But the smaller industries such as boat builders also figure on their list, and Dales keep them supplied with anchor chains and mooring chains.

The company's current directors, Jaqueline Whitehead (who has been associated with Dales for 25 years) and Martin Bradley, attribute Dale's remarkable reputation, even among the giant combines, to their policy of deliberately keeping the firm small enough to give time and personal attention to every customer. And whether they are asked to fill a large order for British Aerospace or to supply strong security chains for bicycles, Dales have built up a reputation for giving a customer just what he needs. They have even been known to provide Roberts Brothers Circus with equipment to tighten up the Czech trapeze artist's wire to exactly the right tension - not to mention supplying them with an elephant-proof shackle!

Providing industry's packing solutions

Con-Lloyd Ltd was first formed in 1924 as C Smethurst Limited, when five members of the Smethurst family invested £600 each and started trading from Heywood making packing cases in which machinery could be safely and conveniently transported from factory to customer, or wherever else it needed to go. To begin with all saws, fastening devices and lifting harnesses were hand operated.

The company was sold in 1956 and the name changed to Lloyds Machinery Packing Company Limited, trading from Princes Street, Manchester.

Ten years later, the Constantine group bought the company, so that there was another change of name, this time to Constantine Lloyd Limited. The current shareholders acquired the business in November 1984. Its present premises at Chapter Street, Newton Heath are the former site of Dempster Engineers and date back to the late 19th century. Heavy gas engineering equipment was made on the site and a great many people were employed in this labour intensive business. Several parts of the original building can still be seen although none of them is still in use.

Machinery of all shapes and sizes is expertly packed by Con-Lloyd for export to all corners of the world. Their clients have included all the leading engineering companies in Manchester and throughout the UK.

Many jobs have been unforgettable, including the packing of a major gas pipeline to stretch some thousands of miles and safely despatched for laying in the USSR. A variety of equipment is handled on behalf of the Ministry of Defence, such as spare parts for submarines, ships and aircraft.

The company is certified by the major airfreight companies at Manchester Airport for the safe packing of hazardous goods.

The facilities at Chapter Street include nineteen overhead cranes with a maximum single lift of seventy tons. There is modern electronic weighing equipment with the facility to weigh accurately items within a tolerance of fifty kilos in 50,000 kilos. It is very important to mark the weight accurately on the packing case so that the correct craneage is used at the docks and on site so that no equipment is dropped and damaged.

In the seventies, the USSR recognised the company as high-quality packers for their goods and issued a certificate to that effect. In those days the USSR had five and seven year plans for purchasing and building capital equipment. Sometimes packing cases would be stored outside in sub-zero temperatures for several years. They needed to have confidence that the packaging for this equipment allowed for the conditions and protected the machinery from deterioration. If Con-Lloyd had packed them, the machines worked as well as they did when they had left the UK factory years before.

In modern business where it is essential to have representatives in all major countries, Con-Lloyd was a founder member of INPRO (International Network of Packing and Routing Organisation). Ted Ashman, the managing director of Con-Lloyd organises and chairs the meetings which are held in a different location each year. Reciprocal trade is encouraged and new packing materials and procedures are discussed.

Although exports of machinery from the UK have been in steady decline since the sixties and despite the increased use of standard metal containers, there is still a need for traditional timber packing cases. By offering a high quality service, Con-Lloyd will continue to be needed in the market for years to come.

Above: A container being loaded onto a vehicle for transporting to the docks.
Top: Complete cases awaiting shipping instructions.
Facing page: Rolls for paper making factory being exported to the USA.

Procter and Gamble - Improving the lives of consumers the world over

In 1833 an English candle maker, William Procter, and an Irish soap maker, James Gamble, married two sisters. Four years later, they formed a partnership which was to become the Procter and Gamble Company.

The company grew quickly and, in the late 1920s, contemplated its first move outside North America. Europe was still getting over the ravages of the Great War and many businesses were going through hard times.

Thomas Hedley, a soap making company based in Newcastle, was such an organisation.

Procter and Gamble took them over in 1930. Many American brands were quickly introduced into the British market. The new parent company's dynamic approach soon saw the Newcastle factory at full stretch so that a new site was needed. Trafford Park in Manchester proved to be ideal. The Trafford Park estates had been on the grounds of Sir Humphrey de Trafford's mansion.

He disliked seeing merchant ships sailing past his property on the newly-constructed Ship Canal and sold the estate!

Eventually the park was sold as lots to any company that wanted to buy. In 1931 ten acres were leased to Procter and Gamble at 9d a square yard and the land was purchased outright in 1933. The original factory took three years to build. It was the largest soap and candle factory in the world and it was officially opened in 1934.

The original products of household soap, candles and scouring powder grew and expanded to reflect the increasing and changing demand of the consumer. New brands were added, new buildings put up and additional land acquired.

By 1959 the company was producing eight times its initial volume and employing 800 people. In 1962 another 23 acres of the park was leased. New brands such as Fairy liquid, Camay and Synthetic granules were introduced to meet the new demands of consumers. Other products such as Lenor and shampoo were moved to Manchester from other Procter and Gamble sites.

Over the last 30 years the Manchester site has changed its product base many times. From Soaps, Edible Oils and Washing Powders, to Shampoos, Conditioners and Disposable Nappies. This reflects the changing needs of the customers, and the Company's ability to adapt.

The new Paper Module opened in 1991 and 650 more staff were taken on. The plant now has three modules; Paper, HABC (Health and Beauty Care), and Distribution.

Today Procter and Gamble are expanding again, with a major installation to manufacture Tissue Towel products. The site employs about 1,000 people and produces more product per person than ever before.

Trafford Park with its road, rail and canal system significantly helps Procter and Gamble with its receipt of raw materials and distribution of finished product.

Procter and Gamble's purpose is to provide products of superior quality and value that improve the lives of the world's consumers. As a result, consumers reward them with leadership sales and profit growth, allowing their people, their shareholders and the Manchester community in which they live and work to prosper.

Facing page: Procter and Gamble's premises at Trafford Park in the early 1930s, then the largest soap and candle factory in the world. **Below:** *Procter and Gamble's huge site as it appears today.*

From Pattern card making to Printing

Where it all began in Central Manchester
H Duffy was established as a printing concern in 1929. Henry Duffy had been a pattern card maker since 1926 but when his son, Mr Louis Duffy, took over, the family concentrated on printing.

The first premises were at 31 Sackville Street, in a room above a confectioner's shop next to the Abercrombie public house. Louis had been working as an engineer in Salford before joining his father to print swing tickets and tag labels which were expensive to buy in.

His first machine was a small Chandler & Price treadle platen which he bought in pieces and assembled himself. He taught himself to produce the firm's stationery, then word spread and orders came in from outside and business began to flourish.

In 1935 Louis Senior married Lillian Williams and, with her support, a second machine was acquired. Before the War, business slackened off and a three day week had to be introduced. At this point came a move to West Mosley Street in the centre of Manchester. During the War, no-one worked there except Louis, his wife Lillian and their daughter Brenda. After the war they were able to take on an apprentice, John Wray, who continued to work for Duffy's into the 1990s. Henry Duffy died in 1947. Under Louis, business continued to prosper with the introduction of three automatic letterpress machines.

The third generation of Duffy's, in the person of Louis junior, studied printing at UMIST, then served two years in HM Forces before working with Tillotsons colour printers of Bolton in 1958.

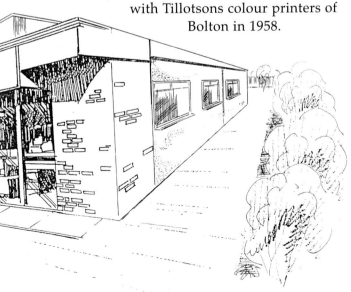

They continued trading in Manchester until 1960 when the business moved to Lower Harriet Street in Walkden, a former bakery. Louis junior joined the firm from Bolton in 1962 and in the same year married Patricia Rogers who became a stalwort with her typesetting abilities. With trade flourishing, the acquisition of the Bank Press, Green Lane, Patricroft, increased the client base and helped establish H Duffy as a recognised commercial printer.

After a fire in March 1976, a severe blow to Duffy's, a compulsory purchase order from Worsley Council forced a move to a disused allotment site by the side of Walkden Cricket Club. Within a matter of months, and whilst continuing to trade, Duffy's built the factory we see today.

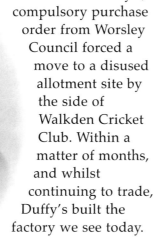

During the 80s the printing industry experienced dramatic changes in production technology. Duffy's incorporated their own design and typesetting facilities with the arrival of two Apple Macs. The 4th generation, Miss Jan Duffy, completed an honours degree at Liverpool University and a diploma in desktop publishing at Blackburn College before joining the firm as a graphics designer in 1988. Once it became 'in-house', Duffy's began to see a rapid improvement in production turn-around. In consequence it bought two two-colour presses and doubled the workforce in less than ten years.

In September 1996 Duffy's held an open day for all its suppliers and clients in celebration of over 70 years' trading in Manchester.

Today, Duffy's continues its progress (begun in 1926) with the introduction of new, larger presses to keep up with increased demand from trade and commercial customers alike.

Above left: The founder, Mr Henry Duffy (circa 1900). Above right: Mr Louis Duffy Senr. (circa 1950). Below: The three partners today - Louis Jnr, Pat & Jan Duffy. Facing page top: Where it all began in central Manchester. Facing page bottom: A sketch of Duffy's today.

Elcometer - getting the measure of the automotive industry

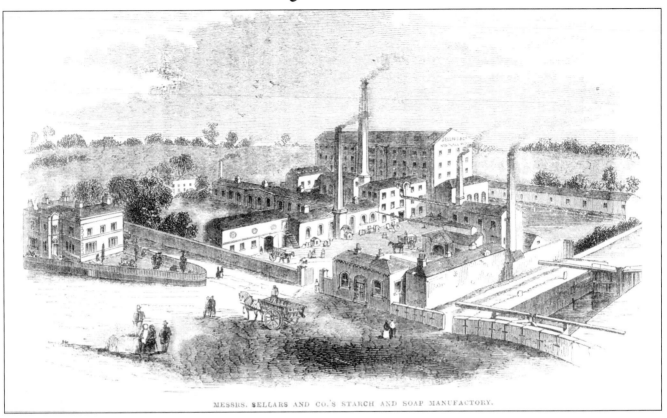

MESSRS. SELLARS AND CO.'S STARCH AND SOAP MANUFACTORY.

Soap and starch. Humble products they may be, but these two basic commodities formed the unlikely starting place for what was to become an international multi million pound instruments company.

It was back in the 1830s that Barratt Carrington Sellars founded a business manufacturing starch and soap, and since then five generations of the family have been involved in the business. Trading as Sellars & Co Starch & Soap Manufacturers, Barratt Sellars's first premises were a complex of buildings next to the canal in the Monsall works, Newton Heath. Five tall chimneys huffed and puffed above the factory while in the busy yard below delivery carts and wagons were loaded and unloaded and, pulled by the firm's patient horses, went out on their various journeys.

Within twenty years the company had become the East Lancashire Chemical Co, and during the 1880s a move was made to Edge Lane in Droylsden where they stayed. A second move in the 1890s took the company to Fairfield Road, which was also in Droylsden. The new premises gave the firm the opportunity to expand their range of products, and they began to make cement as well as soap.

For a hundred years or so the factory's main products remained the same. One of the company's mainstay products was the industrial soap that they manufactured for use in the textile industry. They also made Elco washing soda and colbit, a bitumen emulsion which was used for road building and tennis courts. Colbit was made at the factory until the 1980's. Production of cement ceased at the beginning of the war.

During World War II things progressed as smoothly for the firm as could be expected during wartime, and they even survived a bomb that was dropped on the Fairfield Road works.

After the war John Carrington Sellars, who had taken over the reins of the business, realised with real foresight that the textile industry was not going to survive for very much longer. The knock on effect of that would be a falling off in demand for their industrial soap, and Mr Sellars was concerned.

It was a chance meeting in a radio shop that provided him with the alternative product that he knew the company would need in the future. In the shop he chatted with Jim Hartland, who told him about an idea he had for a product he later called The Elcometer ®, which was an instrument for measuring paint on steel. John Sellars instinctively recognised the potential of the instrument, and without hesitation he offered Hartland a job and went into production. The first of the instruments sold for ten guineas. When asked why a chemical company would make measuring equipment, John Sellars would come back with the comment that ICI made zip fasteners - so why not?

In 1956 the company developed into the electronic instruments. They developed the first transistor instruments in 1960, but sadly John Carrington Sellars died two years later at the comparatively young age of 57.

He would have been thrilled to have been there when in the mid 1970s the company were the first in the world to use micro processors in a coating thickness gauge.

Peter and Ian Sellars took over the business, and in 1962 Ian renamed the instruments side of the business Elcometer Instruments Ltd. From a turnover of £42,000 in 1962, the company developed into today's multi million pound company.

All the manufacturing is still done in Manchester, though today the company owns sales and repair subsidiaries in the USA, Germany and Singapore, with distributors in at least 50 other countries. Their main markets are the automotive, paints and construction industries.

The company's first export order was to Australia in September 1948. Today, seventy percent of their products are exported worldwide, and in 1978 the company won the Queen's Award for Exports, following that with the Award for Technology in 1990. H.R.H. Duke of Kent K G attended Elcometer's 50th Anniversary celebration in 1997. His Royal Highness was a figure familiar to Elcometer; he had performed the opening ceremony for the company's new factory back in 1986.

The original Elcometer is still made in Manchester, though at the same time Elcometer is committed to keeping at the forefront of technology, investing ten percent of its sales in research.

Elcometer's plans for the future are quite simple - to carry on much as they have always done, providing their world of clients with instruments at a price that reflects their commitment to a fair price and allows for new research, new developments - and better products.

Facing page: Original works in Newton Heath M/CR.
Above : An aerial view of the works.
Bottom: Elcometer's 50th Anniversary, H.R.H. Duke of Kent K G with Mr Ian Sellars.

Wire weaving in Strangeways

John Staniar and some of his family founded his wire weaving company in 1790, in the Strangeways district of Manchester. Here they produced mesh using soft annealed wire of various gauges, on wire weaving looms.

By the turn of the century Staniars were established at the Manchester Wire Works in Sherborne Street, Manchester, as mill furnishers. Their factory was extensive and two storeyed with a tall chimney towering over the building. The weaving shed held looms weaving very light meshes up to heavy looms weaving mining wire mesh.

Swiss silk bolting cloth was the mesh used for sieving in the flour mills. Then when nylon became more readily available, this was adopted as a cheaper alternative to silk mesh, and was sold as Nybolt still carrying the trademark "Double Anchor Lion and Cable Brand".

Light plated steel wire cloth was produced exclusively for the flour mills and with their co-operation apertures and free areas were agreed, these remain the same today and

some were woven on hand looms until the late 1950's

We have been dealing with companies such as Spillers, Smith flour mills and various other mills which are now part of Rank Hovis and Allied Mills Groups for over 150 years, with whom we still have excellent business relations today.

The company were awarded medals at the Franco-British Exhibition of 1908 and the Japan-British Exhibition of 1910, for wire mesh, perforated metal

and metal working.

The company was now producing brushes and refilling rolls brushes and sifter brushes, making inlet and outlet sleeves, centrifugal covers, sack trucks, grinder screens and beaters, machinery guards and a vast selection of items for the flour milling and feed milling industry.

An order from a German company was acknowledged on the 2nd April, 1894 and a windmill was then part of the John Staniar logo.

The war years 1940-45 saw materials in short supply when the company had to work to a given quota of materials and production and maintenance were difficult, the building was badly damaged by an incendiary bomb, which hit the works during an air raid on Manchester, the resulting fire was reported by staff who were on fire watch and was extinguished by the fire service.

An aeroplane was built in the factory, the wings being covered by the silk mesh and was one of the first powered flights in the Manchester area, it was known as the 'Staniar Glyder' and a picture of it on exhibition in Heaton park is illustrated.

The company moved to its present site in Stanley Road, Whitefield, in 1989 and in 1990 celebrated 200 years of trading. They are now one of the largest stockists of perforated metal in sheet and made-up screens for grinding and boast a comprehensive range of woven wire and nylon meshes for sieving and every other possible requirement for flour or feed milling.

Above left: One of Staniars first premier purifiers.
Above right: Looking up the mill, how many times has this crane been up and down? *Below:* Silk wings at Heaton Park. *Facing page top:* Gwennie Staniar and father. *Facing page bottom:* The back page of a John Staniar & Co company handbook from 1900's.

Chetham's Library and School of Music

The building in which Chetham's Library and School are housed dates from the early 15th century. Thomas de la Warre, Lord of Manchester and Rector of the Parish Church, (now the Cathedral), obtained a licence from Henry Vth in 1421 to refound the Church as a collegiate foundation. He made over his baronial hall for the purpose but during Tudor times the building was granted to the Earl of Derby. His family kept it until it was seized by Parliament during the Civil War.

Later, Humphrey Chetham, a prosperous 17th century Manchester merchant and landowner, devised a scheme to acquire the property in order to found a Hospital - a school and home for poor boys from the Manchester region and a public library for the use of scholars. Chetham did not live to see his plan accomplished but his executors carried out all his intentions.

In 1564 they acquired the property for £400 and two years later the building was dedicated to its new purpose of a library and school.

Chetham's Library

Chetham's Library is now the oldest surviving public library in the country with a collection of over 100,000 volumes. The library specialises in the history of the north west of England. Notable visitors and readers have included Daniel Defoe and Celia Fiennes, Robert Southey, John Dalton, Karl Marx and Friedrich Engels.

Chetham's School of Music

In 1969 the school was refounded as a specialist music school. Today boys and girls are educated at

Chetham's with the study and performance of music as their specialisation. Concerts are regularly held which all are welcome to attend. Weekly conducted tours are available to groups and societies by arrangement.

Among notable recent successes, four pupils from Chetham's have won the prestigious Audi Junior Musician competition. Thirteen pupils have played in 1998 with the National Youth Orchestra and musicians of international repute frequently perform with the school's pupils. In February 1998 Yan Pascal Tortelier (principal conductor of the BBC Philharmonic Orchestra) was guest conductor of Chetham's Symphony Orchestra and later in that year Lady Walton performed Sir

William Walton's, Facade in concert with members of the school. Pupils from Chetham's have made many broadcasts and recently two CD recordings have been released.

Many pupils leave Chetham's to study at university and conservatoires both in England and overseas. Some pupils choose to read subjects other than music at university and these include english, maths, modern languages and science. Pupils at the school are supported by a Department for Education Scheme for talented musicians. Admission to the school is by audition and no pupil is denied access through lack of funds.

Since its re-foundation as a specialist school of music, Chetham's has occupied a place at the forefront of musical education both nationally and internationally. Former pupils include Peter Donohoe, Daniel Harding, Mike Lindup, Anna Markland and Wayne Marshall. Through musical and academic education, generations of pupils have developed their talents and found fulfilment by being members of this unique community.

*Above: Orchestral studies at Chetham's. **Left:** Chetham's School of Music - a school of excellence in the heart of Manchester. **Facing page:** Chetham's Library - the oldest surviving public library in the country.*

Striving to provide an academic and forward looking education

Manchester High School for Girls has a long tradition of providing an education which is both academic and forward-looking. It was founded in 1874 "to impart to girls the very best education which can be given to fit them for any future which may be before them." Today these aims are maintained by means of a broad range of subjects in the curriculum and by encouraging each pupil to be aware of her own value and that of every other.

The school is indebted for its foundation not to a single benefactor but to the spirit of the times. It was the creation of a body of Manchester citizens, all of whom were convinced of the value of educating girls, providing "for Manchester's daughters what has been provided without stint for Manchester's sons."

The founders of the High School had, as a guiding principle, the value of education as an end in itself, so that, whatever the girls did in the future, they would always be the better for having had it. Many of these prominent citizens belonged to the Manchester Association for Promoting the Higher Education of Women. Its most lasting achievement was the founding of the High School.

Miss Sara Burstall, the school's second Head Mistress (1898-1924), was very influential in its development. She believed in girls learning science - particularly biology - and mathematics, neither of which was commonly studied in girls' schools at

that time. Where the High School undoubtedly led the way was in its Housewifery and Secretarial courses. Miss Burstall had seen Domestic Science taught in the USA and was determined to introduce something similar in Manchester.

Miss Mary Gavin Clarke, who succeeded to the headship in 1924, wrote, "Manchester High School for Girls and its Head Mistress, Miss Sara Burstall, had a legendary fame for me long before I knew the school. It was a pioneer High School for Girls in north-west England and she was a pioneer Head Mistress."

A move was planned from the school's Dover Street premises at the end of the 1920s. The site of a former hospital at Grangethorpe was chosen because of the open land around it despite its main road position. Manchester Corporation gave financial help with the move. At the very beginning of the war, in 1939, the school was evacuated from Dover Street to nearby Cheadle

Hulme. The new school buildings at Grangethorpe, opened in September 1940, were completely obliterated by a German landmine in December 1940. It was not until 1949 that a return was made, in stages, to the school's own premises.

Miss Cottrell's reign as Head Mistress saw new accommodation to provide for the school's increased numbers. The Library was built principally with money donated by the Marks and Sieff sisters and was completed in 1963. A new dining room replaced an old hospital ward. A huge appeal in 1967 raised money for a swimming pool which was opened in 1969. A third storey added to the East Wing made room for more classrooms and a language laboratory. The Preparatory Department was then able to move to Grangethorpe. The great achievement of the next Head Mistress, Miss Blake, was a magnificent new Music House, completed in 1984.

When Miss Blake's successor, Miss Moon, took over, the development continued. A new Entrance was built with a splendid Reception area and Careers suite, as well as new Science Laboratories. Accommodation for the Sixth Form was considerably improved. Under the leadership of the eighth Head Mistress, Miss Diggory, the swimming pool and gyms were refurbished and IT equipment increased throughout the school. Major improvements were made to the Preparatory Department including the building of two new classrooms. Also provided was a new, all-weather hockey pitch which

converts into 12 tennis courts in the summer. Most recently, in the summer of 1998 the School Hall was transformed into a multi-purpose auditorium.

Throughout its history the school's attitude has been progressive and it has kept close, both physically and educationally, to Manchester's universities.

Whatever the future may hold, there is a High School spirit which draws inspiration from a continued tradition of lively minds, enterprise and sound learning. The School moves on towards its bicentenary, full of hope and determination.

Above: An aerial view of Manchester High School for Girls. Below: Girls pictured in the Sara A. Burstall Library. Facing page top: The original Dover Street school pictured in 1923. Facing page bottom: A science lesson in 1899.

Higher education in Manchester

Today's UMIST is ranked sixth university in the country for research, has over six thousand students and has won two Queen's Awards for Higher Education. It is one of only two English universities to have done so. However, UMIST is still at the heart of Manchester, just as it was almost 175 years ago.

The Manchester Mechanics' Institution was established in 1824, entirely through private initiative and funds, to teach artisans the basic principles of science by part time study. The great chemist, John Dalton, was Vice President.

In 1883, John Henry Reynolds, Secretary of the Mechanics' Institution, reorganised the Institution as a technical school. The Technical Instruction Act of 1889, which owed much to the influence of Manchester men, led to taxation providing general financial support for technical education for the first time. The Technical School also benefited much, in terms of land and other resources, through the legacy of Sir Joseph Whitworth and the Royal Jubilee exhibition held in Trafford Park in 1887.

Transfer from the Whitworth Trust to the Manchester Corporation occurred in 1892 and the institution was restyled the municipal Technical School, with instruction provided on four sites.

A period of planning, reorganisation and discussion between the city, the Technical School and the University of Manchester ensued, with fact-finding deputations going to the Continent and to the USA. The building (which now forms the western end of the present Main Building) was begun in 1895 and opened by Prime Minister, Arthur Balfour, in October 1902.

It was within this burgeoning college that the relatively small Faculty of Technology of the University of Manchester for work to degree standard, leading to B Sc Tech and M Sc Tech qualifications, was established in 1905 and this was the forerunner of the modern UMIST.

There then followed the period of the two world wars, separated by the depression and the decline of the Lancashire cotton industry in the 1920s and 1930s. This was a time of consolidation and maintaining links with the City, and one in which the part-time courses were of major importance to the region. Full implementation of plans for an extension to the new building, needed almost immediately after the 1902 opening, was delayed until 1957. Nevertheless ONC, HND and PhD qualifications were introduced and research was revitalised, starting in the 1921-3 period. There was a further renaming of the institution as the Manchester Municipal College of

Technology in 1918. By 1949 over 8,500 students were recruited, most taking non-degree courses.

Dr B V Bowden (later Lord Bowden of Chesterfield) became Principal in 1953 and the great period of expansion of the campus and of disciplines began. In 1955-6 the Manchester College of Science and Technology, as it had become, achieved independent university status, under its Royal Charter, and separate funding from the University Grants Committee.

UMIST is now a major international research university supplying industry and commerce with the graduates they need for the next millennium.

Facing page top: Umist campus today.
Facing page bottom: Cooper Street building in 1825.
Above: Main building 1902.
Below: Main building and environs in the forties.

Electrical equipment for power plants

Now part of ALSTOM, a major international electrical engineering company, ALSTOM T&D Distribution Switchgear Ltd has been manufacturing electrical switchgear on the same site in Higher Openshaw since 1913. ALSTOM manufactures and supplies a complete range of equipment, systems and services for the generation, transmission and distribution of electricity from the power plant to large-end users. Formed in 1989 through the merger of the energy and transport activities of GEC and Alcatel Alsthom, ALSTOM can trace its origins back to the earliest steam power plant and locomotives.

Towards the end of 1913, a partnership was formed between Samuel Ferguson and George Pailin, both previously employed by Ferranti Ltd. The partnership's business was the manufacture of switchgear. The two-man team had small resources but tremendous courage and determination. Ferguson Pailin had capital of £1,000 and premises of 189 square yards in Edward Street, Higher Openshaw.

The first order came from the Stalybridge Electricity Undertaking. and was for wall type isolator cubicle units. Switchboards were all different and so there was no standard production line. Nevertheless there was a satisfactory profit on the first year's trading and by 1918, Ferguson Pailin & Company Ltd was floated with capital of £200,000.

An Edward Street Works extension was completed in 1918. Work continued to come in. Manchester Corporation Electricity Department ordered switchgear to be installed in the Dickinson Street Substation which was completed in 1924 This was among the first 33kV 'vertically isolated' switchgear to be commissioned in Great Britain. Similar equipment was supplied to the North Wales Power Company.

In the late twenties the company amalgamated with several other electrical firms to form Associated

Above: Ferguson Pailin stand at the British Empire Exhibition, Wembley in 1923.

Construction of this was under way in 1925. Over the years additional facilities were added. A woodworking shop where pattern making, the manufacture of packing cases and general joinery work was carried out. A boilerhouse was commissioned in 1954 to supply the factory with heat and steam pressure for various processes. A bar stores was built, followed by a pump house, a hydraulic test bay, ambulance and library buildings, a canteen, various extension bays which provided more factory floor space and a garage.

Electrical Industries Limited *(AEI)*. Within this group the company retained its identity and continued to manufacture electrical switchgear. Electricity was a rapidly growing industry and, then as now, the Ferguson Pailin organisation kept abreast of developments, increasing the variety of its products and components manufactured. It also invested in its own high-voltage and mechanical testing facilities, a rare achievement for an individual company at the time and a major factor in subsequent switchgear development.

Ferguson Pailin was a leader in the development of metalclad switchgear with its inherent benefits in operation and safety.

The continuing growth in the business encouraged the company to embark on a policy of expansion. An adjacent site in Buckley Street was purchased for the building of a new main works and offices.

The social responsibilities of employers to their employees had not been overlooked. Ferguson Pailin showed an awareness of the value of welfare work by their practical support of worthwhile activities. In 1939 they purchased Mottram Hall, a spacious country mansion in 130 acres of parkland as a holiday home for employees. It had comfortable accommodation and recreational facilities that were fully used and greatly enjoyed. A thriving Social Club embraced many activities including football, bowls, cricket, shooting, chess and a male voice choir.

Above: Transport - 1925.
Below: The Factory - 1922.

The period following the Second World War was more one of improvement and consolidation of established lines in an increasingly competitive environment rather than one of radical change in products. It was a demonstration of the company's commercial acumen and engineering ability that the Higher Openshaw factory continued to find markets for its products in the sixties which was a time of unprecedented contraction of the industry in the UK.

In 1959 the company name was changed to Associated Electrical Industries Limited (AEI). The rationalisation which followed the merger of AEI, the General Electric

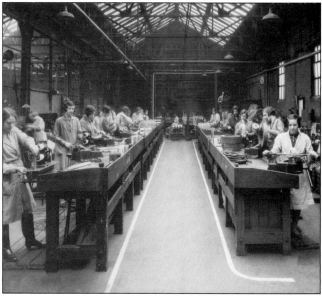

technical and commercial expertise for which it had become renowned.

In the seventies it emerged as strong as ever as the leading British manufacturer of medium voltage distribution switchgear. This was the decade of changing technology, with the use of vacuum interrupters in place of oil circuit breakers leading to improved products with simplified designs and reduced maintenance requirements. In 1973 GEC Distribution Switchgear celebrated its diamond jubilee with the introduction of BVAC, an innovative design of switchgear and one of the first in the world to use vacuum interrupters.

In the late eighties came the merger of the GEC power businesses with those of Alcatel ALSTHOM to form GEC Alsthom which, ten years later in 1998 became ALSTOM. Since its formation the Company

Company (GEC) and English Electric in 1967 and 1968 led to the site being selected as the centre for the development and manufacture of the medium voltage businesses of the enlarged GEC group.

It was an acknowledgement of the worldwide reputation that the company enjoyed and the

Left: 33kV units under construction in 1927
Above : Ladies at work in the factory in 1927.
Below: Training school - Apprentices in 1945.

has continued to advance, expanding both geographically and in terms of its products and services. It has also built a reputation as an innovator, through its ability to anticipate customers' needs, not only with its technology but also through its service and financing solutions. Today ALSTOM is one of the world's leading suppliers of components, equipment, systems and services to the power generation, transmission and distribution, rail transport and marine markets. The Company is

known for its high speed trains which operate on numerous routes in Europe at speeds of up to 300km per hour. Its power plants are helping the development of economies worldwide.

ALSTOM serves the world's markets by drawing on a wide range of expertise. These skills have been developed from a large installed equipment base. They include the management of complex projects, risk control, cost management, research, development and design, world class manufacturing and innovative financing.

These capabilities bind the Company together. Alongside the Company's technical knowledge, they have made possible a range of improved products and services that anticipate change, meet the ever more complex needs of their customers and provide superior performance. From giant hydroelectric power plants in Brazil to high voltage substations in Egypt, from high speed rail systems on three continents to the world's largest airport handling centre, the Company's expertise is helping leading businesses to remain at the forefront of their industries.

As part of a major international company, ALSTOM T&D Distribution Switchgear Ltd continues in its role as a leading designer and manufacturer of medium voltage switchgear, which it sells to power generators; electricity, gas and water utilities; oil, petrochemical, steel, paper and industrial users; rail and marine customers, both at home and around the world.

And so, today, ALSTOM T&D Distribution Switchgear Ltd, with a worldwide market for its products, continues the tradition of enterprise, innovation and excellence established on the Higher Openshaw site in 1913 by Ferguson Pailin.

Above: Works Open Day, 1948
Left: New offices, 1956.
Facing page above: Assembly Area, 1920's.
Facing page below: Assembly Area, 1990's.

The hidden history of Market Street

The Arndale Shopping Centre is one of the busiest and largest indoor, city centre based shopping complexes in Europe but, underneath its many acres lies a forgotten part of Manchester's Medieval history. Originally, Roman, Saxon and Norman communities lived around the river banks where the Irwell and Irk converge. By 1301 Manchester was granted a Royal Charter. At that time Withingreave Hall, a large, half-timbered house with its surrounding grounds, existed on the site.

In the 1700s, Market Stead Lane, as Market Street was then known, was changing rapidly to a commercial area. Many of Manchester's wealthy and famous residents lived in the area and the continuing name of Cromford Court, then off Market Stead Lane, was the home of Sir Richard Arkwright, the famous inventor.

In 1820, it was considered that traffic congestion was a problem! At its narrowest point, Market Street was only five yards wide and was regarded as the most congested street in Europe. In 1822 an Act of Parliament was passed to buy up properties and widen the street.

Over the next ten years Manchester lost the major part of its Medieval architecture. At this time the markets began to move from their original, overcrowded sites in the market place to more spacious areas of Shudehill. The whole area between Market Street and Withy Grove became a maze of tiny passages and thoroughfares which were ill-lit and without drainage. Manchester's population quadrupled to 360,000. Corporation Street was built in 1845 as a direct route from Market Street to Withy Grove.

And now?
The Arndale Shopping Centre was built between 1972 and 1976 but the first site was purchased in 1955. Negotiations with Manchester City Council merged its holdings with those of the Town &

This picture: *Barbirolli Mall, Manchester Arndale Centre, 1998.* ***Facing page:*** *Cromford Court, Manchester Arndale Centre, 1998.*

City Development Company and agreement was reached for the whole area zoned for redevelopment to be leased to Town & City.

In 1968 a site was designated as part of the 26-acre redevelopment. Between then and 1970 there were negotiations to re-house traders already on the site in the new scheme. Where possible, they were given continuity of trading. In October 1969, the Ministry of Housing and Local Government approved the planning application submitted by Town & City Development, so that the first Compulsory Purchase Order could be confirmed in April 1971. In May of the following year, Taylor Woodrow commenced construction on the site. In the next January, Building Agreement and Agreement for Lease were exchanged with Manchester City Council and the Prudential Assurance Company.

By June 1975, Burtons, Thomas Cook and Dunn & Co. were amongst the first relocated tenants to begin trading. A year later the Phase 1 Mall was opened with 60 shops including stores for W H Smith and Mothercare. This was followed by Knightsbridge Mall, later to be re-named Voyagers Walk, Phase 2 North and Phase 3 South which included Boots, the Market Hall and the Pedestrian bridge link to Marks and Spencer. Phase 4 opened in 1979 and included major stores for British Home Stores and Littlewoods. The bus station, catering for an estimated 40,000 passengers opened at the same time. Finally, in May 1979, came the official opening by HRH the Princess Royal.

In the years between 1987 and 1995, Phases 4 to 8 were completed and opened. The scope of the finished Centre is 15 acres comprising land north and south of Market Street and Cannon Street, both streets being bridged by enclosed shopping malls. The architects were Hugh Wilson and Lewis Womersley.

"THE MANCHESTER ARNDALE CENTRE IS ONE OF THE LARGEST CITY CENTRE BASED COVERED COMPLEXES IN EUROPE"

The Manchester Arndale Centre is one of the largest covered city centre based shopping complexes in Europe with an average of 750,000 shoppers passing through every week. It boasts a wide choice of the very best shopping facilities with over 230 shops and stores.

A rolling refurbishment programme ensures that a high standard of design is maintained and retailers are encouraged to refit to an equally high standard. There is an effective management team which contributes to the Centre's strong customer loyalty. Access to the Centre could not be easier with a 1450-space car-park and with Metrolink, Victoria and Piccadilly British Rail Stations adjacent to the shopping centre.

The Centre is going from strength to strength as it repositions itself as the focal point in Manchester's plans for a major remodelling of the city. When the IRA bomb exploded in June 1996, Manchester Arndale Centre had already begun a massive refurbishment programme. This included reroofing and the installation of new atria allowing natural daylight into the Centre creating a fresh and welcoming atmosphere for shoppers. The part of the Centre seen from Corporation Street is undergoing a massive transformation as it opens shop fronts out on to the pavement. The Prudential Assurance Company, in consultation with its partners, has developed the strategy for the Centre to ensure it retains its position as one of the UK's busiest shopping centres. The first phase of the new work centres around the elevation to Boots on Cross Street. The design is contemporary whilst being sympathetic to the traditional Manchester surroundings. This face of the Centre will be replaced with a modern look designed by the Ratcliff Partnership. It incorporates stone, red brick and granite, complemented by the use of more modern materials. There are metallic panels, planar glazing, glass blocks and light-weight, high-tech steel and glass canopies. The use of this design will continue down Corporation Street, adding relief and interest to the building.

A glass and steel tube bridge is to span the distance between Marks & Spencer's new store and the remodelled Arndale Shopping Centre. This bridge is the first of its kind in the world and is an hour-glass-shaped spiral of steel and glass with a timber walk-way for shoppers travelling between two buildings. This structure, achieved by using ground-breaking technology, has been designed by the architects, Hodder Associates, in consultation with structural engineers, Ove Arup.

It is hoped that future phases of the development will include tenants trading from Corporation Street, (opposite M&S), bringing more life into the area.

In addition to the new developments, the demand for retail space is as strong as ever and the UK's busiest shopping centre looks forward to creating a better shopping experience than ever before.

Facing page: Hallé Square, Manchester Arndale Centre 1998.

Last train to the Exhibition Centre

The last train from the Central Station, Manchester, left at 11pm on May 5th 1969 to Warrington. It had served Manchester well for almost 90 years as the northern terminus for the Cheshire Lines Committee Railway that later became the LMS.

Deserted by trains and passengers, 'Central' became the subject of one speculative property deal after another. The British Rail Properties Board had plenty of potential offers for 26 acres of prime inner-city land with its substantial buildings but they all disappeared when the property bubble burst in 1973.

That year British Rail sold the entire 'Central' site and buildings to a Jersey-registered firm called Arkle, (who owned the race horse). Manchester City Council was outbid on this and various other occasions as the site continued to change hands.

Meanwhile Central Station was ravaged by vandals and the weather, and fell into major disrepair. In 1977, structural repairs were made to prevent the buildings collapsing, but only absolutely essential work was done. Then, in the following year, GMC's Chief Executive persuaded Commercial Union to become joint redevelopment partners for the site.

Together they organised a year-long venture study to find a practical solution to the site's development. It had to integrate existing listed buildings and plan for new ones. It was decided to convert the listed Train Hall into a national-standard exhibitions and events centre. Around it there was to be a hotel and residential accommodation, together with leisure and recreational facilities. Suggestions for these included a sports complex with an ice rink, shops, offices, bars, restaurants and craft workshops or buildings for other job-creating businesses.

The attractive scheme, in its first phase at least was welcomed by both partners and, after considerable lobbying, the UK Government and the EEC both agreed to help fund the £21 million Exhibition Centre. Work was begun in the summer of 1983.

Thanks to the work done in 1977, the Train Hall was structurally sound, though very decayed. Community enterprise teams from the Manpower Services Commission had renovated the extensive vaults in 1982. Conservation experts such as the Royal Fine Arts Commission and the Victorian Society were consulted before the final designs were agreed on.

had a stylish new roof on the original 'Paxton' lines with glittering glazing inside the iron work. Under this a single exhibition hall would provide 110,000 square feet of uninterrupted floor space. This could be divided when necessary by means of floor-to-ceiling 'sails'.

Much of the existing blue and pink brickwork would be restored. Often it needed dismantling

As much as possible of the character and detail of the original was to be kept, including eighteen massive iron arches supporting the vast, single-span roof and the glazing on each gable-end. Jack Bogle's creation

*Above: A side view of the G-MEX Centre. **Right:** Just one of the many exhibitions that have taken place at the G-MEX Centre. **Facing page:** The spectacular front aspect of the G-MEX Centre.*

and rebuilding, brick by brick. The station's original iron platform columns were reused to support the all-new glazed entrances, bars, restaurants and side walkways. Where the ironwork had disintegrated moulds were made to produce identical new castings.

The Undercroft consists of deep, brick-lined vaults, forming a labyrinth that runs the length and breadth of the building. This provided a place to put the extensive servicing ducts and space for car parking.

Central Station had been built immediately over the Junction Canal so that road, rail and canal networks converged on the one spot. Today, part of that 150 year old canal bed forms part of the new underpass access route to G-Mex's underground car parks. Elsewhere beneath the Centre a section of the original waterway remains, though it can be reached only at the end of a long inspection chamber.

The completed G-MEX Centre is distinguished by striking steel and glass-walled main entrances. Bars and offices have glazed, tent-shaped roofs, sculpted to tone with the original gabling. The centrepiece of the northern main entrance is the splendid old railway clock, now restored to working order for a second century stint. When it was dismantled in 1983 a 'time capsule' was found in the mechanism, a metal casket

containing documents and small items of Victoriana. The southern end of the building is the more imposing, its elevated location showing it off to their best advantage the sweeping spans of the Centre's roof.

Inside G-MEX visitors and exhibitors have the benefit of the most modern heating, lighting and ventilation systems. The bars and restaurants, and the cloakrooms have creature-comforts to match and there are all the ancillary exhibition services any user could expect. The proof of the exhibition centre is in the booking, to misquote a well-known proverb. G-MEX was soon well-

Above: The entrance to the seminar centre.
Left: Another exhibition taking place in the main exhibition area of the G-MEX Centre.

proven. In the nine months following the opening in March 1986, twenty seven exhibitions took place. In the following year it was virtually a sell-out with back-to-back exhibitions during the busy periods.

The Centre was, and is, patronised by exhibitors of furniture, computers, business, fashion, travel and building to mention but a few. Particularly popular with the people of Manchester are the Holiday and Travel and the Motorcycle Shows.

Alongside the marketing, the events side of the calendar has been running. World superstars have appeared in the Arena/Auditorium which seats eight thousand. Programmes of music have been as varied as classical and a Pop Prom season and top tennis, show jumping, boxing, soccer, athletics and ice spectaculars have entertained audiences.

Today's patrons would do well to spare a thought for those whose efforts achieved this impressive transformation.

The Manchester architect, Jack Bogle spent a whole year "just getting to understand the form and shape" of the historic building before beginning the daunting task of turning a redundant railway terminus into a practical but exciting exhibitions complex and enhancing an already-spectacular example of Victorian grandeur.

Project Manager, Malcolm Reece, and Management Chief, John Ball, had the formidable role of synchronising the activities of dozens of contractors, scores of suppliers and hundreds of workmen in their combined efforts for three whole years and then produced the finished result on time!

These men summarised the attitudes of all the people concerned in the venture, 'belief, co-operation and commitment.'

Below: An atmospheric night-time view of the illuminated G-MEX Centre.

150 years in tune with the world of music

In the nineteenth century, two young brothers James and Henry Forsyth, were apprenticed to the "Prince of Pianomakers" Broadwood in London. They were working under their father, who was the factory manager. James and Henry were the third generation of the Forsyth family to be associated with the then great house of Broadwood. The two young men, however, while keeping links with Broadwood, were about to break with family tradition.

It was 1857, and the Art Treasures Exhibition, staged in Manchester, was attracting many visitors to the city. The celebrated pianist and conductor Charles Hallé had formed a 60 member orchestra to give concerts at the Exhibition. Following this success, Hallé decided to move from Paris to Manchester and asked the Forsyth brothers to join him in Manchester to look after his pianos and manage the business affairs of his orchestra. The outcome was a partnership which was destined to become legendary in the city of Manchester and in the world of music. The brothers set up business in the old Kendal Milne building on the corner of St Anne's Street and Deansgate originally retailing, hiring, tuning and repairing only pianos. Managing the Hallé Orchestra was mainly James Forsyth's concern. In the 1880s the firm moved to their current premises in Deansgate.

In addition to organising orchestral concerts and smaller classical recitals (the latter often in their own concert room), the Forsyths acted as agents for many performers, singers, comedians, magicians and even circus artists. The firm's reputation, however, was built on music, and encouraged by a growing number of customers, they gradually increased their range of goods and services to include sale and repairs of all orchestral instruments, sale of sheet music and books about music, and hire of teaching studios.

James and Henry Forsyth were not slow to take advantage of every opportunity and encouraged once again by Charles Hallé they diversified into music publishing setting up a publishing business in London to publish his piano teaching method. This was followed early in the twentieth century by the famous piano teaching music of Walter Carroll (first music advisor to Manchester City Education Department). How many pianists first began with "Scenes at a Farm"? In the 20s and 30s, Forsyths

with five floors dedicated to all kinds of musical products. Their activities are diverse, exporting pianos to Nigeria, Music to Holland and the Far East, recordings to Guyana and Japan, and their customers include not only both pop and classical musicians but music teachers, schools, hotels and restaurants. They number among their customers many famous artists including Manchester United players Eric Cantona and Nicky Butt, golfer Ian Woosnam, conductor En Chou and well known personalities Phil Collins, Lisa Stansfield, Victoria Wood and *Take That's* Mark Owen.

branched out again adding sales of wireless, gramophones and records. During the depression sales were often so slow that James' grandson, who was now in the business and had started the gramophone department, would buy a box of needles to prevent the till showing nil for the day.

The company rode out the two world wars and it was during the first war that they started to employ women although it was the men who did the fire watching from the roof during the second war!

From its earliest origins to the present day Forsyth's has been a true family firm. James Forsyth's son Algernon followed him into the business becoming a director and working every day until three weeks before his death at the age of 98 in 1961. Henry's son James Aikman Forsyth worked with the firm in Manchester from where he took over the management of the Hallé Orchestra. He went on to become music critic on the News Chronicle and the London Star. Algernon was joined by his nephew Kenneth Howes and today, Anthea (a Forsyth great grand daughter) and Robin Loat run the business with their son Simon.

The forties saw the addition of record making facilities followed in the fifties by television and hi-fi. In the seventies the music publishing business was moved to Manchester and due to the redevelopment of the next door premises they had previously occupied, regretfully the teaching studios and concert/rehearsal room were closed ending rehearsals at Forsyth's for the cast of West Side Story, Hair, and Covent Garden touring opera.

Based on their firm belief in good quality and variety of choice the company's success continued

In the 1980s the company diversified further, starting up a wholesale piano business importing German pianos. Still moving with the times, they began to stock not only acoustic but electronic keyboards and guitars, even automatic traditional pianos.

Robin Loat puts the success of the company down to a number of points: their determination to keep abreast of modern developments and trends, the fact that they carry a huge range of stock under one roof for customers to compare and choose from - and their reputation for offering sound and honest advice and quality goods at competitive prices.

It is with this formula that, for almost 150 years, Forsyth's have developed and maintained a unique and enviable reputation throughout the world of music.

And Forsyth's plans for the future? To continue with this winning formula with even more effort.

One thing the music-buying public can be sure of both now and in the future: whatever customers are likely to demand, Forsyths will be sure to keep in stock.

Above: A view of a section of the piano showroom today.
Facing page top: James Forsyth one of the founding brothers. Facing page bottom: A competition winning window display in 1926.

Blooming flowers in a growing business

The business of Messrs Ernest Broadbelt Ltd, the wholesale fruit and flower merchants and commission agents of Smith field Market, Manchester, began in quite a small way. However, from the beginning there has been continual expansion.

In 1947, a booklet was published as part of the celebration of 50 years of trading. By then the warehousing space covered four acres and included some accommodation for railway rolling stock in its yard and interiors. At Oldham Road LMS goods yard, some of the best warehouses in the fruit trade were controlled by the firm. They had been specially built to deal with the large volume of overseas fruit and they possessed direct railway delivery with facilities from quick distribution to all parts of the country. Its telegraphic address, 'Vitesse', epitomised the company's alertness. Both directors, Mr Ernest Broadbelt and Mr Stanley Butters, were in constant attendance at the Smithfield Market premises.

In the late forties the cut flower department became increasingly important and the company became one of the largest flower distributors in the North of England. Mr Broadbelt travelled widely and was well known among growers and shippers in all parts. The company was a member of the National Federation of Fruit and Potato Traders' Association and was one of the largest distributors of the then famous 'Blue Label' brand of Fyffes bananas. There was a magnificent banana ripening room at their Oldham Road warehouses so that the fruits were kept in the best possible condition.

Mr Broadbelt died in 1952. He had no family and left the business to Stanley Butters who had served him loyally for many years. Mr Butters' son and one of his daughters worked in the business.

Part of a consignment of Lettuce from F.A. SECRETT

Sadly, the son was killed in service, on D-Day, so that Mr Butters had to continue working in the company right until his death in 1958. His grandsons joined the business in the seventies and they are currently in charge of it.

Today's refrigerated vans, forklift trucks, pallets and pallet trucks are a far cry from the handcart, horse and cart and ladders that were standard equipment when the business first began. It has always been a good firm to work for, so that a good many staff have stayed for their whole career. Their bankers (Midland) and accountants (Joseph Crossley & Sons) have been equally loyal, both having served since 1897.

The company is the only importer in the UK of fresh bilberries, continuing a link with the Polish people started by Ernest Broadbelt. Nowadays Broadbelts' main customers are secondary wholesalers and caterers as they are supplying fewer and fewer retailers due to supermarkets destroying the high street. Nevertheless, their reputation for reliability and the freshness of their products means that Broadbelts are still flourishing. They celebrated their centenary in 1997 and are looking forward to their next hundred years' trading in Manchester.

Facing page top: Mr Ernest Broadbelt, Governing Director. *Facing page centre right:* Mr Stanley Butters, Director. *Facing page bottom:* Lettuce and greens transported on horse and cart, a common sight at the beginning of Ernest Broadbelts business venture. *Above:* Ripening rooms where the famous "Blue Label" brand of Fyffes bananas were ripened. *Left:* Stephen and Philip Dewhurst.

Helping to shape the Manchester of today

In 1876 Mr Thomas Till and Mr Frederick Whitehead opened an ironmongery and mill furnishing business in a converted Victorian town house on the corner of Chester Road and Egerton Street, Hulme

The business grew so that within a few years the other four houses in the block were converted into shop and warehouse premises. It was from the varied stock carried by Till and Whitehead that general ironmongery, contractors' tools, picks and shovels were supplied for the construction of the Manchester Ship Canal. In fact, throughout its life, the company has been connected in some way with every major project in the Greater Manchester area, including the motorways, railways and the international airport.

It was noticed during the early 60s that the building was beginning to lean into the road. Then the site was included in a designated slum clearance area. Things looked bleak with the prospect of the company's buildings being demolished.

Soon afterwards the Ministry of Transport proposed the building of a flyover, the Mancunian Way, so that the company was obliged to vacate its premises. The Hulme site was being redeveloped for light industry and the argument then ensued about

whether Till & Whitehead fitted into this category went to litigation. Eventually the company was granted a site.

In 1966 there was a move to larger modern premises in Ellesmere Street, Hulme. The contract for designing and constructing the new building went to Atcost.

In the new building specialist departments were created to deal with Builders' Ironmongery, Industrial Fasteners, Electric and Hand Tools, with a separate department to cope with the ever-increasing demand for Steel-slotted Angle Shelving and Speedframe Units.

The company also became distributors in the Lancashire and Cheshire area for Camping Gaz products and other butane, propane appliances for the leisure trade and for industrial users.

In 1976 the Company Centenary was celebrated with a dinner at the County Cricket Ground. The toast was, 'Our customers, past present and future and our many friends in the trade.'

Today, Till & Whitehead boast a 16,000 square feet warehouse with over 20,000 products. They have a busy, active trade counter offering friendly technical advice across a diverse product range. They also offer technical support sourced from years of trade experience.

The product range the company offers spans hand and power tools, architectural ironmongery, fixings and fastenings, adhesives and sealants, personal protection and workwear, ladders, janitorial products, shelving and racking, brushware, security products, cutting tools and abrasives, to mention some of them.

The company supplies to local authorities, hospitals, hotel groups, property companies, universities, store groups and so on. Airports, engineering, utilities and transport are recent areas which have provided the company with new customers.

Thanks to competitive pricing, knowledgeable staff and a next-day delivery service, business is good and expected to increase in the next century.

Above and facing page, bottom: Two aspects of Till and Whiteheads premises at 86-94 Chester Road.
Facing page, top: The scene shortly after a three ton lorry carrying cement crashed into the shop in July, 1952.

"THROUGHOUT ITS LIFE THE COMPANY HAS BEEN CONNECTED IN SOME WAY WITH EVERY MAJOR PROJECT IN THE GREATER MANCHESTER AREA"

Haddock, Herrings and Halibut - the compleat history of Wilde's

Ten-year-old Joseph Wilde owed much to the fact that customers on his coal round enjoyed a meal of fish and chips at lunchtime.

It was the late 1800s, and the young boy was helping out the family by driving a coal cart; it was obvious even at that young age that here was a young entrepreneur who was destined to go places! Joe's lunch was often a bag of fried fish and chips, and he would eat them while he made his deliveries. His customers, who faced a long walk to the nearest fish and chip shop, envied Joe his tasty dinner, and often told him that they wished they had someone to deliver fish and chips to them. He was to remember their comments in later years.

During the time he spent on the coal cart Joseph formed an affinity with horses. As he grew older he became a jockey with Crumps Stable of Trotting Horses, and raced at Manchester Race Course. After some consideration, however, he arrived at the key decision not to carry on in the racing business.

Instead he started up in business selling wholesale fish, poultry and game at the old Smithfield Market in Manchester.

The venture was a success and before long the whole family - his wife, son Joseph and brother Vincent - all became involved.

Joe Wilde the third, Wilde's present proprietor, remembers that his father bought and filleted fish ready for the fish fryer; it was Uncle Vinny's job to sell the flat fish while Granny did the weighing and looked after the money. A nice bit of 'finny haddock' was a popular meal, and the family smoked their own haddock and cod in Edge Street Smoke House, which interestingly was converted into an ice maker in the 1920s.

The family's hard work paid off and during World War One Joseph did well and was even able to put money in the bank. The economic climate of the twenties was no picnic, however, even for a well-established firm, and Joe unfortunately lost out, finding himself back at square one. But he rode the tide and the fishmonger's business survived and went on to prosper.

The market traders were a close community and when the old wholesale fish market closed its doors for the last time in 1972 it was a sad day for all, particularly for the Wilde family, who had been at those first premises since the first Joseph Wilde founded the business back in 1900. The old building was later demolished, leaving only the decorative main gate with its decorative panel showing the Bible story of Christ's disciples fishing on the Sea of Galilee.

The move to the new Smithfield Market at Openshaw brought its own difficulties, but the firm continued to flourish. Joe Wilde the second took up the reins from his father, and in turn passed on the business to his sons Joe Wilde the third and his brother Brian.

Today, fish is not abundant as it once was, and though the present Joe Wilde still sells salmon, prawns and fish, much of the fish is now farmed. He is now finding chicken a worthwhile alternative, and he finds his markets largely among Indian tandoori restaurants and takeaways, Chinese wholesalers and fast food outlets. He imports from countries almost worldwide - Italy, Holland, New Zealand, Australia, Brazil, India and Thailand - and his customers, many on local markets, range widely across the north of England and into Wales.

When Joe Wilde is not selling fish, he is developing his other keen interest - painting pictures. Joe is recognised as a very talented artist, and he has become well known in the local area, where his pictures are exhibited regularly.

Thanks to the hard work of all the family, Wilde's fish and poultry business survived the 1990s slump that hit traders hard, and is still healthy.

The biggest blow to them has been the growing popularity, through the 1980s and 1990s, of huge supermarkets and Indian food outlets. The trend towards out of town shopping has meant the closure of many of the small shops once supplied by Smithfield Market, devastating the wholesale market traders. Over 50,000 shops once served by Smithfield have now shut down.

But Joe Wilde the third, like his grandfather, is a hard worker and a born survivor. He - along with the rest of the family - is determined that Wilde's will not merely carry on but will grow and expand in the years to come.

Above: The Wilde family.
Facing page: One of Joe's paintings of the Smithfield market in the 1960s.

Over a century of entertainment at the Palace Theatre & Opera House

Apollo Leisure have owned both the Opera House and the Palace Theatre in Manchester since 1990 but the history of the theatres goes much further back.

The Palace Theatre, a venture organised and funded by directors, promoters and interested persons, opened in May 1891. The Palace had to open dry because, owing to lobbying from the Wesleyans, no liquor license was granted. Even though the inaugural performance was a ballet, 'Cleopatra', they feared the Palace would be a 'den of iniquity'.

In all, three ballets were put on, all resulting in substantial losses. The management sensibly decided at that point to give the customers what they wanted, Variety! Success soon followed when Charlie Chaplin, Vesta Tilley, Little Titch and Harry Lauder topped the bill.

In 1898, the Biograph, an early version of cinematography, played between the acts. A modest pantomime, Jack & Jill, was presented in 1907, which marked the beginning of the Palace as the shrine of 'Panto' in the north.

Then in 1912 the New Theatre or Opera House opened on Boxing Day with a production of 'Kismet'. This was a huge success. The Palace's response was to engage Bertie Crew, an eminent London theatre architect, to reshape and refurbish its premises. It reopened in December 1913 complete with 'luxury tip-up seats' and got straight back into the business it knew best, Variety. Artists now included Harry Houdini and Eustace Gray's Palladium Minstrels.

Meanwhile the New Theatre was not doing so well with its revised programme of cinema, circus and tea dances. It was sold to United Theatres Ltd in 1915. Then, in the following year, Sir Thomas Beecham brought his opera company to the New Theatre, which in 1920 became the Opera House.

Both theatres flourished during the First World War as people tried to distract themselves from the real issues of the day. The Palace put on revues and full length musicals with performers who became household names and included Sophie Tucker, Gracie Fields and a young John Gielgud.

1929 saw increased competition from the 'Talkies', and the Palace retaliated with Noel Coward's 'Palace Lives' starring Gertrude Lawrence, the legendary Laurence Olivier and Noel Coward himself.

The Opera House was sold to the Howard & Wyndham chain in 1931. Once the war was over, great names such as Edith Evans and Peter Ustinov played there and the European premier of 'Oklahoma' took place there in 1947.

In 1939 the Palace Theatre gave Vera Lynn her debut and launched the voice that was to epitomise wartime entertainment. During the forties the Palace played host to Arthur Askey, Max Wall and Laurel & Hardy. This type of entertainment was hit hard by television in the fifties and so the Palace went right back to its opening ploy of putting on ballet, together with some opera, musicals and straight plays.

The Opera House followed 'Oklahoma' with other musicals, including 'West Side Story', for which the stage was reinforced to accommodate the energetic dancing.

In January 1959 Moss Empires stopped supplying the Palace with shows and after a short struggle to remain independent, it became a subsidiary of the Moss Empires and was used as a 'try-out' house for London-bound productions. The Opera House had continued success with 205 performances of 'My Fair Lady' while other productions starred Fonteyn, Nuryev, Albert Finney and Marlene Dietrich.

Over the following years it became obvious that it was only financially viable to run one theatre. Manchester had to decide which should be funded and saved. Eventually the Palace Theatre was chosen because of its potential for expansion. The Opera House closed in 1979 and, sadly, became a bingo hall.

A great future was now seen for the Palace as one of Europe's largest and best equipped centres for the performing arts. Rebuilding and refurbishment at a cost of £4 million was done and the Palace reopened in 1981 with a gala performance of 'Jesus Christ Superstar' in the presence of HRH the Prince of Wales. In 1984, thanks to the vision of Bob Scott, of the Manchester Palace Theatre Trust, the Opera House reopened as a sister venue of the Palace. More than restored to its former glory, it opened with 'Barnum' which was attended by HRH the Princess Anne. The company which owned both theatres, Manchester Theatres Ltd, was bought for £7.2 million by Apollo Leisure and many major touring shows now visit both theatres. The Palace Theatre broke box office records in 1992-93 with its 13 month run of 'Les Misérables', which was followed by the hugely successful,'Phantom of the Opera' at the Opera House. The future is far from bleak for them now.

Above: Inside the Palace Theatre this beautiful interior still remains from the beginning of the century.
Left: Oxford Street, Manchester circa 1942.
Facing page: Palace Theatre, Oxford Street, Manchester in the 1890's.

Success based on secret ingredients

Generations of ancient tradition have produced the secret recipes used in the kitchens of the Yang Sing Restaurant in Manchester's Chinatown.

Founded by celebrated Dim Sum chef T K Yeung and his wife in 1977, the Yang Sing quickly established itself as an eating-house of repute. The Yeungs' own reputation for producing the very best in Oriental food had already been established back in Hong Kong, before the family moved to the UK.

Carrying on the family tradition, their son Harry Yeung became the Yang Sing's head chef, and his brother Gerry, restaurant manager. Mr and Mrs Yeung supervised the general running of the business. Originally situated in George Street, the restaurant was first opened as a private business, becoming a limited company in 1983. The Yang Sing quickly gained a reputation for all-round excellence, and is now recognised by many as one of Europe's leading Cantonese restaurants.

Since those early days the Yang Sing has undergone a number of changes - not all of them welcome. In October 1997 their establishment was unfortunately destroyed by fire, and at the worst possible time. Christmas bookings had already been taken, and the management was suddenly presented with the enormous problem of catering for thousands of clients over the festive season. They found a solution in hiring part of the G-Mex Centre and importing their diners lock, stock and barrel.

History and traditional Cantonese recipes have played their own part in the continuing success of the restaurant. The secret recipes that went into carving out the Yang Sing's reputation are not this restaurant's only secrets, however; pride of place goes to the outstanding talent of 'Mr Harry', as Harry Yeung is affectionately known to regular clients. As the establishment's head chef, he is responsible for taking the best of Oriental ingredients, putting them all together and creating the distinctive flavours that have made the Yang Sing famous.

Mr Harry is one of the most celebrated chefs in Europe, and he has combined the accumulated experience of many generations of the Yeung family with his own outstanding skills, enabling him to produce what can only be called culinary masterpieces.

From the outside, the restaurant looks very much like any other elegant Victorian building in this vibrant Chinatown community, and apart from the fragrant and mouth-watering odours that tempt one inside, its only identification is the long banner that proclaims that this is the Yang Sing. Step through the doorway, however, and you will find yourself in a whole new world.

The city of Manchester itself has key connections with university life, business, commerce and industry and the Nynex Arena - not to mention Old Trafford and Manchester United football team! It is situated centrally to a network of motorways and rail routes, and has its own international airport. The aim of the Yang Sing has long been to provide facilities that cater for the wide range of needs that its position in Manchester's commercial centre demands, whether they are business meetings held over dinner or lunch, families marking a big

*Top: A beautifully carved serpent. **Above:** Staff proudly display food for a banquet. **Left:** A busy restaurant.*

occasion, couples celebrating an anniversary over a quiet and intimate dinner or large and formal banquets.

Prior to the fire the Yang Sing provided for the needs of every type of client, the restaurant had three dramatically contrasting floors, each with its own identity.

The basement restaurant had an atmosphere that was uniquely its own. There, the focus was on the family celebration or the lunchtime business meeting or entertaining an important client at dinner. Sixty of Mr Harry's famous one-day specials complemented a menu of more than 300 exceptional dishes.

The first floor had seating for more than 200 diners, and was available for the exclusive business banquet, while the second floor's authentic Beijing setting offered the kind of privacy and comfort that is perfect for a more intimate private party. The restaurant is at present operating from its temporary home at Charlotte Street until the original restaurant is fully restored by April 1999.

In this exotic atmosphere, Mr Harry and his team use only the best and freshest of seasonal ingredients (many imported from Hong Kong) and an assortment of traditional Chinese woks and kitchen equipment to create rare and unusual dishes that even those in the know about Chinese food have never heard of.

When 34 Princess Street is fully restored the famous basement restaurant will be re-instated virtually as it was, there will be a small ground floor restaurant, the first floor will be two separate smaller banqueting rooms and the second floor a

large banqueting room for up to 250 people.

The Yeung family firmly believe that eating out should be unforgettable, a fun time that will provide customers with an interlude from the calls of everyday life, and their main aim has always been to give their clients an experience that will stay with them for a long time. They see their advantages as being the human rather than the technical element, and their entire management team extends to clients the hospitality that is unique to the Chinese, attending to their needs with speed and efficiency. The Yeungs are not content to sit back and rest on their laurels, however. The opening of fast food outlets at the new out-of-town Trafford Centre is among their ambitious plans for the future that will take the Yang Sing forward into the next millennium with flying colours.

Top left: Master Chef and company Chairman Harry Yeung. Top right: A lion on the prowl at the opening night of the restaurant's temporary premises on Charlotte Street. Below: Managing Director Gerry Yeung (left) with two guests on the same evening.

A Belle Vue circus parade during the Second World War

ACKNOWLEDGMENTS

CHRIS MAKEPEACE, HISTORIAN

MANCHESTER CENTRAL LIBRARY: LOCAL STUDIES UNIT

MANCHESTER CITY FC

MANCHESTER UNITED FC

LEN MYATT